Expatriate Entrepreneurs

IN EMERGING MARKETS

Ten Success Stories
from Argentina

David English

EXPAT
BOOKS

MENDOZA
ARGENTINA

EXPAT BOOKS

M E N D O Z A
A R G E N T I N A

EXPAT–BOOKS.COM

Photography: Federico Garcia

Design and Production: THINK Book Works

ISBN   978-0-615-50760-6

A Dedication

I might never have moved to Argentina, started my own business, and written this book if it were not for the example set by my father, Bill English. He was a direct-mail copywriter back in the days when spam arrived in your mailbox rather than your inbox and wrote fund-raising letters for every television evangelist from Earnest Angley to Jim Baker and Oral Roberts.

Dad wasn't exactly proud of his work, but it did generate great stories. One day after a luncheon meeting, he accompanied the founder of a leading Christian television network out to his car. As the preacher sat down in a brand-new Mercedes-Benz convertible, he looked up at my father with a sly grin and said, "God's been good to me." That's about the time my old man decided to stop working with TV evangelists and become an entrepreneur.

Nonetheless, many of Dad's new ventures still had a religious angle. Having grown up in the Methodist Church, it was the world he knew. One summer he subjected the family to driving around the back roads of Arkansas and Tennessee to tape sample bags of fortune cookies containing Bible verses to every church door we could find. Since we went out at night, the police often showed up to chase us out of town. Occasionally, the pastors called us to order a few boxes of "scripture cookies." More often than not, it was to complain that the tape on the sample bag had ripped the paint off the front door of their chapel. Needless to say, it wasn't a very profitable business. My brother, Steven, and I were still eating stale cookies with scriptures inside when we went off to college ten years later.

Another year, we helped Dad proofread copies of his book, *The Backpacker's Bible*. The idea was that religious-minded folk would want to have the Good Lord along with them when they hiked the

Appalachian Trail. I think our mother still has three or four boxes of those bibles out in the garage (next to a huge bag of scripture cookies).

Then, there were the "Ain't Jesus Great" license-plate frames. Dad sold them wholesale to churches for only one season, but for years afterward we would spot them on cars around town. To our parents' chagrin, the letters cracked and peeled off over time. This produced results such as "A n us eat" and "A t eat" that were hilarious to my brother and me.

To be fair, these dubious entrepreneurial adventures were interspersed amongst my father's successful endeavors. A book he wrote on being an entrepreneur was used as a textbook at several universities. He developed highly successful fund-raising campaigns for the United Methodist Church. And he launched a small market research firm that performed qualitative research for nearly every major magazine publisher in the United States, as well as such newspapers as *The Wall Street Journal* and *The Washington Post*.

What I learned from my father was the value of persistence and a positive attitude. No matter how badly one of his projects turned out, he picked himself up and started over again. He just kept trying until he hit on something that worked. I never heard him complain even once about a failed venture. Right down to the bitter end in the nursing home, even through the fog of Alzheimer's disease, his response to "How are you doing today, Dad?" was a genuinely enthusiastic "Great!" By example, he taught me to always look to the future and to never miss an opportunity to start fresh. Those are two qualities critical to being an entrepreneur and, as it turns out, a writer. That's why this book is dedicated to my father, William Merlin English.

Contents

Introduction

"Go West, young man, and grow up with the country."
—JOHN B. L. SOULE

We live in an era of economic uncertainty for major industrialized nations. It's also a time when developing countries need creative entrepreneurs to propel growth and modernization.[1] This combination of factors represents an extraordinary opportunity to "go West," to move to a place like Argentina where the cost of living and the cost of starting a business are relatively low, and where a foreigner's unique skills and perspective are a competitive advantage. This book is about individuals I know who did just that, including myself. We are expatriate entrepreneurs in an emerging market, and our success stories reveal the fundamental lessons on what it takes for someone from North America or Europe to start a business in the developing world.

---

1. Since no single definition of *developing country* or *emerging market* is recognized internationally, in this book I use the terms interchangeably. The definition I most like for both, and which is certainly relevant to Argentina, can be found in *Winning in Emerging Markets: A Road Map for Strategy and Execution*, by Tarum Khanna and Krishna G. Palepu. They write, "Emerging markets reflect those transactional arenas where buyers and sellers are not easily or efficiently able to come together. . . . Institutional voids make a market 'emerging' and are a prime source of the higher transaction costs and operating challenges in these markets."

Why This Book

At the end of 2001, I was greatly concerned about what was happening in my country and around the globe. Because I worked in New York City's financial district, I found myself at Ground Zero on the morning of September 11. (See Chapter 1 for more on this.) My experiences on and immediately after that day had affected me profoundly. So had a business trip I made earlier that same year to General Electric's medical division in Milwaukee, Wisconsin. There I witnessed firsthand what Thomas Friedman would later write about in *The World Is Flat*: Indian software engineers in the United States on temporary visas, four to a hotel room, doing work previously done by Americans, at a fraction of the cost.

In part because I saw ominous signs of drastic change on a global scale, and in part because I had spent time in Argentina and knew it held great potential, I decided to become an entrepreneur in an emerging market. Today I own an investment consulting firm in Mendoza, Argentina; help run several of the city's business clubs; organize cultural and educational exchange programs; teach classes at local business schools; and actively participate in Mendocino society. Moving to this country has been a wonderful experience and the key to my personal and professional success.

In my office I regularly receive foreigners who have fallen in love with Argentina and are thinking about starting a business here— executives like the "old me" who sense that globalization threatens their livelihood at home but offers opportunities abroad, university students who want to build a career in the developing world, and investors considering new projects. My experience helping so many people reach their goals has enabled me to identify what is required for a foreigner to succeed as an entrepreneur in Mendoza, in Argentina, and in an emerging market. That's why I wrote this book.

Whom You'll Meet in These Pages

Moving to another country in pursuit of opportunity is not a new phenomenon, although historically it has often been attributed to fleeing a

war zone, persecution, or an economic crisis. What is new is the growing number of relatively wealthy people who are actually *leaving* what
immigrants of previous generations considered "the promised land."

From the United States alone, there has been a big rise in the
number of citizens living abroad. According to the U.S. State
Department, there were 1.5 million expatriates in 1990, but nearly
8 million by 2009. In part, this is because it has become easier and
more popular to retire to countries like Mexico and Costa Rica.
However, it's also because the developing world is now the true land
of opportunity for a certain kind of person.

You would think that an individual trying to build a company in
a country with a different language, culture, and business environment would be at a big disadvantage. To be sure, it's not easy. But the
stories in this book demonstrate that it's possible to overcome the
obstacles and succeed by capitalizing on what makes you stand out
from the crowd.

I'm going to introduce you to men and women of various nationalities and backgrounds. They include an Irish playwright turned
magazine publisher, an American entrepreneur who runs a multifaceted wine and vineyard real estate enterprise, a French financial
consultant reborn as a restaurateur, a Harvard-educated architect
from Mexico who operates a rural boutique hotel, a big-dreaming
mother and tour operator from California, a French woman raised
in the Ivory Coast who runs a book-publishing company, a Spanish
investment banker who founded one of Argentina's most prestigious
wineries, an American Hungarian couple who export the world's
only Malbec vodka to the United States and Europe, and a Chinese-
speaking Parisian who sells European winery equipment throughout
Argentina.

These expatriate entrepreneurs have a lot in common. They are
hardworking risk takers who love adventure and thrive on challenges. They are open to new ideas and new ways of doing things.
Wherever they come from, they don't think it is unequivocally the
"best country in the world." They believe that people have to find
the places that are best for them, based on who they are and what

they want out of life. That may be the town in which they were born or on the other side of the planet.

Many started businesses in Argentina because they knew they had the skills to serve a need in a specific industry—a need they were able to identify thanks to relevant experience gained in their native countries. Others started businesses because they could "be somebody" here they could never be back home—a big fish in a small pond. Some made the move simply because they wanted to be a pioneer in a land that still has wide-open frontiers. While each person who has shared his or her story is a unique individual with a different personal history, as a group they teach us much about the attitudes, motivations, and business philosophies that are essential to doing business as a foreigner in a developing country.

Why These People

I chose to interview the ten expatriate entrepreneurs in this book not only because they have compelling tales to tell but also because they:

- Have operated a business in Argentina for three years or more
- Have a reputation for ethical business practices
- Are considered successful by peers in the community
- Have received press coverage in local and foreign media
- Are of diverse nationalities, backgrounds, and industries

I established these criteria for three reasons: (1) to be able to draw conclusions from a wide variety of personal stories; (2) to assure readers that the people I interviewed own reputable, ongoing business concerns; and (3) to demonstrate that their success can be independently verified by multiple sources (the media, peers, current or former clients, etc.). In other words, I wanted the lessons in this book to be relevant for readers regardless of their home countries or the type of venture they were contemplating. In addition, it had to be a good bet that in five to ten years the expatriate entrepreneurs I interviewed would still be in business. After all, long-term success is what proves the credibility of a company and its founder.

Why Me

In 2003 I founded a consulting firm with the mission of guiding investors from overseas through the many pitfalls of doing business in Argentina. Since then, I have helped hundreds of people start companies here. As president of the Mendoza Expats Club, I presided over the birth of a community of expatriate entrepreneurs in an emerging market. I do have an MBA from Austral University in Buenos Aires; yet, it was my hands-on business experience that most helped me pinpoint the lessons in this book. My long-standing relationships with most of the people I interviewed gave me great insight into the evolution of their companies.

As the author of this work, I leveraged my direct knowledge of the businesses and the people running them to ask revealing questions, edit the responses, and draw relevant conclusions. I put the same twenty-five questions to each entrepreneur, ranging from "How have you been able to overcome the challenges of language and culture to be successful in a developing country?" to "What's your secret of success in general?" To craft the questions and know how to ask them, I drew on my past experience performing qualitative market research for business publications such as *Forbes* and *BusinessWeek*. My objective was simple: tell each entrepreneur's story and, in doing so, highlight the main reasons for his or her success. Using a standard list of questions and asking them in a specific order was vital to achieving this goal and ensuring the integrity of my work.

To be clear, this is not intended as an academic analysis or a step-by-step handbook.[2] It is a collection of inspirational stories with

---

2. I have not taken an academic case study approach in this book, because doing so would require more statistical and financial evidence of success than I have included here. Several considerations led to my decision to present the stories in the more narrative form. First, privately owned companies have no obligation to disclose their financial data. Second, in a highly regulated and bureaucratic environment business owners hesitate to give specifics that might attract the attention of government inspectors. And third, the stories in these pages demonstrate that personal success is measured by much more than just the hard numbers of a business.

"big-picture" lessons followed by a summary of critical success factors. If I've done my job well, you'll find that *Expatriate Entrepreneurs in Emerging Markets* is a fitting companion to the many how-to publications that cover everything from business strategy in emerging markets to banking and work visas.

Why These Lessons

Some of the lessons in this book may seem repetitive or obvious. But certain lessons bear repeating, especially when they are taught from different perspectives and accompanied by clear examples of how they have been put into practice. This is because the lessons of success often conflict with human nature.

Over the past ten years, I've seen that people who are competent professionals back home often make commonsense mistakes when doing business in Argentina. They start big rather than small. They fall in love with a property, an investment opportunity, or an idea, shutting out those who are more knowledgeable about the local environment and may offer constructive criticism. They jump head-first into a new venture without finding a more experienced partner (or they choose the wrong partner altogether). They don't seek the advice of honest and independent experts. They try to transplant their ways of doing things to a developing country without taking the local culture into consideration.

Much can be learned from the individuals in the following pages because few of them succumbed to these tendencies, or if they did succumb, they recovered. In fact, the common elements in their stories explain why, as a group, they have been successful where so many others have failed. That's why their lessons, however familiar, are so important.

Why Mendoza

This book is the first in a series to spell out the lessons of North American and European entrepreneurs who started businesses

Although the stories in this book are set amongst the vineyards of Mendoza, their lessons are applicable to other emerging markets.

in specific emerging markets. I began with Mendoza, Argentina, because it is where I have lived and worked for the past decade. Also, Mendoza is home to hundreds of entrepreneurs from around the world. It therefore serves as a good example of the type of environment in which they flourish.

It isn't a new idea to examine a single community of people in order to identify lessons that can be applied in other cities or countries. One well-known study demonstrating this idea was conducted by health professionals in the 1960s. They interviewed a group of unusually healthy Italian Americans living in Roseto, Pennsylvania, where the death rate from all causes was 30 to 35 percent lower than the national average. Researchers discovered that the citizens of Roseto were healthy due in large part to the quality of their relationships, their involvement in civic organizations, and their sense of community. It turned out that the ways in which people in a specific town were beating the odds were relevant to human beings everywhere.

I have been careful to focus on reasons for success that are not unique to Mendoza, so that the lessons in this book are applicable to other parts of Argentina and to other emerging markets, just as the lessons from the Roseto study are applicable to healthy living in any town. For example, there's no doubt that Mendoza's booming wine industry has played a role in many of the following success stories. However, I don't suggest relocating to a city where wine tourism is taking off. Instead, I recommend identifying places where one or more industries have the potential for rapid growth following a significant change in the political or economic environment. This way, if you have the background and skills to provide goods or services related to that industry, you'll be positioned to succeed. This approach has been well proven in places other than Mendoza. It worked for entrepreneurs in Hollywood in the early twentieth century; for their counterparts in Prague, Czechoslovakia, in the 1990s after the fall of the Soviet Union; and for others in Bangalore, India, which in the past decade has become a major high-tech center.

Remember: An entrepreneur in another location that shares some of Mendoza's attributes will have a better chance of success than in a place that shares none of them. With that in mind, let's now examine the setting for the stories you are about to read.

Prologue
MENDOZA, ARGENTINA

"You are stealing our best people."
—AL GORE

hen former U.S. Vice President Al Gore visited Mendoza in October 2009 for a conference on climate change, I introduced him to a number of Americans who live in this city. He was so surprised to see us here that in his keynote address he accused Argentina of "stealing our best people." The comment was a hit with the locals and featured prominently in most press coverage of the event. Everyone wanted to know what was luring so many *yanquis* (Americans), as well as other foreigners, to this part of the world.

A Land of Opportunity

Most recently, entrepreneurs have been drawn to Argentina by currency devaluation and a drastic reduction in real estate values. In 2001, the Argentine government defaulted on US$81 billion of sovereign debt (the largest such default in history) and went through four presidents in ten days. Almost overnight the cost of a cup of coffee in Buenos Aires dropped from three U.S. dollars to one. The value of nearly all other goods and services fell by that much if not more. Top-end vineyards in Mendoza that previously cost $15,000 per hectare (2.47 acres) suddenly became available for less than $5,000 per hectare—and *everyone* was selling despite the fact that a

Pristine air, water, and soil have attracted investors to Argentina for centuries.

hectare of similar vineyard in Napa, California, was worth as much as $300,000. As large, foreign-owned corporations fled the country, individual investors seized the opportunity. Nine of the eleven expatriate entrepreneurs in this book (including myself) moved here immediately following the crisis. Nearly all of them say the low-cost operating environment they encountered at the time was critical to their success.

In addition, many who are concerned about global conflict and the natural environment are attracted by the fact that Argentina is located in the southern hemisphere. With only 10 percent of the world's population and a much smaller percentage of its industrialization, this hemisphere is the purest, cleanest, and safest half of the planet. Since global air currents run mostly west to east, pollution, radioactivity, and airborne viruses are distant threats. If you are unlucky in this country you will find yourself in an earthquake, not a war zone.

Argentina also has an abundance of natural resources and some of the most fertile farmland on the planet. This is one reason why North American and European corporations in the cattle and grain industries have been doing business here for well over one hundred years. It also explains in part why so many foreigners have moved to this nation since its founding in 1816. Although the predominant culture in Argentina today evolved from Spanish and Italian immigrants, English, French, German, Middle Eastern, Irish, and even Welsh arrivals have also left their mark.

Along with strong European influence, Argentines share a common heritage with most other Latin American countries as well as cultural traits that are found in many parts of the developing world. Foreigners living here often comment on employees who lack corporate loyalty, businesses run by people whose only qualifications are their last names, customers who accept that standing in long lines is normal, and a lack of customer service to the point that some business owners act as if clients are a nuisance. Of course, these traits can actually attract expatriate entrepreneurs. After all, they give individuals from other cultures the chance to be especially competitive here in certain lines of business.

Interestingly, the expatriate entrepreneurs I interviewed for this book told me many times that what they most like about Argentina are the Argentines. Argentines often allow their emotions to get the best of them when driving, negotiating, or boasting about what they have (Argentines are known as braggarts in the rest of Latin America thanks in part to the *porteños* from Buenos Aires who, like New Yorkers, are known for being brash). But they are equally uninhibited when cheering at a soccer match, kissing on a park bench, dancing until dawn at a nightclub, or spending the entire day with the family at a public park. In fact, the Argentines have a great saying that sums up their zest for life: "They can't take from you that which you have already danced." It's a contagious attitude and one reason so many foreigners fall in love with this country and its people.

Michael Evans, CEO of The Vines of Mendoza—a private vineyard estate enterprise, tasting room, and wine shop—explains, "Argentines are passionate about everything they do. You meet a winemaker like Carmelo Patti and you say, 'This guy is doing this because he loves it, not because he wants to get rich or impress his friends with a 100-point wine.' The opposite is what I too often felt in Napa."

In short, when Al Gore said Argentina was "stealing our best people," he should not have been surprised. Whether because of low operating costs, clean air and water, abundant natural resources, distance from global conflicts, or the Argentines themselves, Argentina has often been and is today a land of opportunity for people from all over the world.

A Progressive City

Say the word *Argentina* and most people immediately think of Buenos Aires. It's true that in recent years this vibrant international capital, with more than 14 million inhabitants and a passion for the tango, has become a mecca for investors and tourists alike. But Buenos Aires, a sea-level city with access to the Atlantic Ocean, is only

Mendoza is a city known for its cleanliness and beauty, as well as a strong sense of community.

one part of the Argentine landmass, which comprises nearly three million square kilometers (more than one million square miles).

Mendoza, which is the name of both the province and the city, is about 1,000 kilometers (600 miles) due west of Buenos Aires and another world entirely. Similar in terrain to Denver, Colorado, Mendoza sits high at 750 meters (2,500 feet) on a desert plain at the edge of the Andes, a tremendous range of snowcapped mountains. The skies are crystal blue nearly three hundred days out of the year. At night, the stars shine with a brightness not seen in many parts of the world for one hundred years. The air and water are fresh. The soil, when irrigated with mountain snowmelt, is ideal for crops such as the grapes that are used to create world-class wines, as well as peaches, pears, plums, tomatoes, garlic, and onions. It is not by coincidence that one of its satellite towns is named New California.

Because Mendoza is much closer to Santiago, Chile, than to Buenos Aires, exporters of fruit, vegetables, and wine have their choice of deep-water ports near one city or the other. When I sent a container of antique furniture to the United States, I chose the Port of Valparaiso in Chile, which is fewer than 500 kilometers (310 miles) from Mendoza. It took half the time to get there and was less expensive and less risky than Buenos Aires, whose Port Authority is known to be more bureaucratic.

The city's location is perfect for tourism and industry. Since its founding in 1561, Mendoza has been the main stopping point on the road over the Andes between Santiago and Buenos Aires. That's why in 1923 a grand hotel, casino, and concert hall were built adjacent to the city's main plaza. The complex, now the Park Hyatt Mendoza and the Teatro Independencia, remains a focal point for Mendocino elites as well as affluent foreign tourists. For good reason, many of the expatriate entrepreneurs profiled in this book have their businesses physically located within ten blocks of it.

Due to an earthquake that destroyed the city in 1861, Mendoza no longer has the typical colonial Spanish layout or architecture. Its streets are wide and lined with tall, leafy trees. There is a large central plaza surrounded by four smaller ones, each with a unique theme that is a nod to the city's heritage. Parque San Martin, one of the largest and most beautiful parks in South America, sits on Mendoza's western perimeter. Hundreds of small coffee shops line the city's streets, with tables and chairs placed on the sidewalks to take full advantage of the spectacular climate. On the Paseo Peatonal Sarmiento, a pedestrian mall in the city center, Mendocinos and visitors alike enjoy a coffee, a beer, a glass of wine, or a meal as they meet with business contacts or check e-mail on Mendoza's free Wi-Fi network.

Despite the greater metropolitan area's population of just over one million people, the capital contains only about 115,000. Somewhat like a "little Manhattan," Mendoza is divided into distinct commercial districts or sections. Most of the computer stores are concentrated in one area, the clothing stores in another, and the bookstores in yet another. Many locals come on foot or on cheap public transportation from the outlying neighborhoods to do their shopping in the lively downtown district. In this sense, Mendoza must be similar to many U.S. cities before suburban sprawl and strip malls sucked much of the life from their vibrant centers.

Within Argentina, Mendoza is known for being a particularly clean and well-organized city. The locals take great pride in that reputation and are adamant about maintaining the appearance of their community. Victor Fayad, the city's mayor from 1987 to 1991 and again from 2007 to 2011, is credited with doing what it takes to maintain Mendoza's image as a progressive municipality. His accomplishments include overseeing construction of the city's main pedestrian mall, purchasing a new fleet of waste collection vehicles, turning an abandoned rail yard into a park and cultural center, and initiating a major repaving program. As a result, Mendocinos tend to address him affectionately as "Viti," rather than as "Mayor Fayad."

In terms of higher education, Mendoza boasts no fewer than seven universities. The renowned Universidad Nacional de Cuyo, with its schools of medicine, law, economics, and agriculture, is considered one of the best tertiary institutions in the country. Mendocinos are

Public plazas and parks help to make Mendoza one of Argentina's most livable cities.

also committed to self-improvement. Many take language, art, or speech classes at one of the private institutes that dot the city. This means that expatriate entrepreneurs who live here can count on a highly educated workforce to help them build their businesses.

A Traditional Society

Although Mendoza is a progressive city in many ways, its citizens are socially conservative. Mendocinos feel so tightly bound to their friends and family members that few ever move away for work or study. Their time-honored traditions such as *asado* (barbecue) cookouts, *mate* (tea) parties, and *truco* (playing card) nights serve to reinforce existing cliques. As a result, it can be difficult for newcomers, even those from neighboring provinces, to integrate themselves into Mendoza's traditional society.

Helene Chevalier, owner of Millesime S.A., a distributor of European winery equipment, says it's not that the locals are unfriendly; it's just that they will ask you over to dinner once to be polite, but probably won't do it again. "In Mendoza the people move in closed social circles. When I first arrived, the locals invited me

Mendocinos follow time-honored traditions such as drinking *mate* with close friends and family members.

out. But they soon stopped calling. It wasn't anything personal. I just didn't fit in," Helene explains. To put this in perspective, think about how you would feel if you organized a family reunion and your cousin brought a strange friend who spoke with an accent, couldn't follow a conversation, and didn't understand a single inside joke. In short, introducing someone new into their established groups makes Mendocinos feel uncomfortable.

Nonetheless, the most successful expatriate entrepreneurs here have managed to break the ice with the locals. How? By taking the initiative and hacking away, little by little. From the beginning, nearly all of Michael Evans's staff at The Vines of Mendoza was Mendocino. He created a sense of family by hosting barbecue luncheons every Sunday to show that he and his company were committed to this city and its people. "We wanted Mendoza to know that we were not flying in, making an investment, getting out, and waiting for it to pay off. We are here for the long haul and want to be part of the society," says Michael.

Once they've broken the ice and adapted to living here, foreigners tend to love the Mendocino lifestyle. Tour operator Carolyn Gallagher moved to Mendoza in great part because of it: "Here it's less commercial than in the United States. You close the door to your business on Sunday and have a three- or four-hour lunch with your family. You slow down, and you have social time. It's not, 'Consume! Consume! Consume!'" Carolyn also appreciates that there is less emphasis on getting high. "Growing up in California, I was always exposed to drugs and alcohol. Mendocinos drink, but they almost never get drunk. It's a healthier society."

Even though Helene Chevalier arrived in Mendoza thinking she wouldn't stay for more than a few years, she now says, "I can't see myself ever leaving. Part of the reason is that Mendocinos put so much emphasis on personal relationships." And Michael Evans remarks, "I love that I know the butcher down the street better than I knew my next-door neighbor in L.A. Despite the initial standoffishness, there's still much more of a sense of community here than in the States." Ironically, in a traditional society some would call "closed," many entrepreneurs from overseas feel more at home than ever before.

What's Next

You're about to meet a group of men and women who bet their futures on their creativity, adaptability, and personal courage. How did they identify and take advantage of opportunities in an emerging market? What factors explain why they succeeded where so many others have failed? What lessons can be learned from their success stories?

The next eleven chapters will answer those questions.

Phoenix

"The phoenix hope, can wing her way through the desert skies,
and still defying fortune's spite; revive from ashes and rise."
—MIGUEL DE CERVANTES

t was a bright and sunny walk to work. Exiting the subway station, I looked up at the sun above the skyscrapers and thought, "This is going to be a great day." At 10:30 A.M., I would meet with top executives at CitiGroup's corporate headquarters to close on a wireless Internet implementation—the culmination of a year of hard work and the justification for my job as a technology consultant at Qwest Communications in New York City.

On my way uptown, I stopped by my office across from the famous statue of the stock market bull on Lower Broadway to pick up some papers. I rolled my eyes when Eric, a salesman in a nearby cubicle, started yelling, "Holy shit! Holy shit! Holy shit!" as the elevator doors closed to take me back downstairs. It sounded as if he had won big on one of his overnight stock trades.

By the time I reached the street, ashes were already falling like early winter snow. So were documents that hadn't burned, many emblazoned with "Extremely Confidential." Of course, no one was bothering to read the private documents blowing in the wind along the curb. Most people were looking up at one of the Twin Towers and asking how some idiot private pilot could have crashed his Cessna on a beautiful day like today.

19

Because my meeting at CitiGroup was absolutely crucial to my gainful employment, and because New Yorkers were accustomed to a range of accidents and catastrophes for which business was seldom canceled, I went uptown without giving it a thought.

When I entered the subway station at Wall Street, I left one world. When I came up from the station at 51st Street, I entered a very different one. Within twenty minutes, I had become that *Twilight Zone* astronaut who returned from a brief spaceflight to find an "Earth" where everything was turned upside down.

Thick black smoke rose ominously in the southern sky; a woman hysterically screamed "I love you" into a cell phone as tears ran down her face; a hugely obese man in a three-piece suit sprinted north while looking nervously over his shoulder and shouting unintelligibly; fire engines and ambulances raced toward an abyss; and people scrambled over one another to withdraw cash from any ATM in sight. It was complete pandemonium.

In the CitiGroup conference room where I was to have my career-clinching meeting, the executives were gathered around a large television tuned to the *Today* show. Together, we watched the end of the world as we knew it. Events would take a while to run their course, but my precious deal and my career were effectively over as of September 11.

Be Motivated

2001 was a turning point in my life. That year the realities of globalization hit me like a one-two punch. First, on a business trip to GE Healthcare in Milwaukee, I saw that large corporations were importing low-wage workers from the developing world to reduce their labor costs in technology, and the U.S. government was issuing temporary work visas to enable the practice. Second, September 11 drove home the fact that where I was living and what I was doing there made me particularly vulnerable to sociopolitical and macroeconomic forces beyond my control.

As 2001 came to a close, there were two things I couldn't ignore: the memory of the Indian programmers I had met in Milwaukee and the growing piles of newspapers at my neighbors' doorsteps when I returned home every night from the office. Many of the people in my apartment building were never coming back from Ground Zero, and neither were many of the jobs being outsourced overseas. That realization motivated me to reassess my life and move to a place where a person with my background and education could best compete in the flat world of the twenty-first century. Although I wouldn't leave the United States for several more years, 2001 was the seed of my eventual rebirth as an entrepreneur in an emerging market.

My personal story is perhaps more dramatic than most. Like the "phoenix hope" of Cervantes, I literally rose anew from fire and ash to defy fortune's spite. Yet, every expatriate who chooses to start a business in a country like Argentina and sticks with it long enough to be successful does so because he or she is strongly motivated by *something*. After all, it is not natural to tear oneself from the comfort of native language and culture, as well as friends and family, to live and work in an alien and initially daunting environment. Think about what motivates you to become an entrepreneur in an emerging market and ask yourself how committed you are to the journey. As the motivational speaker Les Brown says, "Wanting is not enough. You must hunger for it. Your motivation must be absolutely compelling in order to overcome the obstacles that will invariably come your way."

Learn the Language

When I graduated from the University of Tennessee in 1995, I went to work for Cano Ozgener, who had immigrated to the United States in the 1950s to study engineering. When he saw an opportunity to import Meerschaum pipes from his native Turkey, Cano left his job at DuPont and opened a small office in the basement of his home in Nashville. As it turns out, my first boss was an expatriate entrepreneur.

Cano didn't have a lot of money at the time, but he did have vision and the conviction that creative young people were key to the success of his business. So Cano hired my best friend, Jim Yarbrough, and me to start his cigar division, despite our having no idea what we were doing. It was great working for him because Jim and I were able to do things for which we had no experience and no qualifications. Cano gave us the wonderful opportunity to *learn*.

One memorable learning experience occurred when Cano sent Jim to Nicaragua to oversee the manufacture of cigars as well as several thousand cedar cigar boxes. After he returned home, Jim assured us that all had gone very well. So, when several huge UPS packages arrived at the office, Cano enthusiastically tore them open to inspect the contents. Unfortunately, the "boxes" were more like bricks. The dimensions were perfect, but the boxes were solid rather than hollow. As Cano took the first box out of its packaging, he shouted in his trademark Turkish-Tennessee accent, "My God! These are not boxes; these are treeeeeeees!"

Obviously, there had been a terrible misunderstanding between Jim and the people in Nicaragua. The incident was my first experience with the pitfalls of doing business overseas and underscored the importance of clear communication in a multilingual environment. That experience and others since then have taught me that before moving to an emerging market, an entrepreneur should learn the basics of the native language and *keep studying*. Unless you are one of those lucky people raised in a bilingual family, there's always room for improvement. Enroll in classes or hire a private tutor to minimize the risk that a slip of your tongue will lead to an embarrassing and costly mistake.

Keep It Simple, Stupid

To his credit, Cano Ozgener supported me fully in January 1996 when I proposed to sell his CAO brand cigars into the Japanese market. In Tokyo, I ate strange food (like fish-flavored ice cream with scales as a topping) and washed it down with a lot of strong sake. I also closed a deal to sell Cano's cigars to Tsuge Pipe Company. This was the first step on my path to becoming an entrepreneur in Argentina.

During my visit to Japan, the president of Tsuge Pipe showed me the Zippo lighter cases his company made. He asked if I could create something similar in Nashville from the wooden cuttings usually thrown away in the manufacturing process of Gibson guitars. Sensing an opportunity, and having learned not to be intimidated by a complete lack of experience, I answered with an affirmative "Hai!"

With the help of Toshinari Ishii, the Japanese External Trade Organization (JETRO) representative in Nashville, I developed a prototype and submitted a proposal to Gibson's licensing director, Joe Anielo. To my amazement, my proposal was accepted. I was barely twenty-five.

Naïve and overly ambitious, I made the mistake of starting off complex rather than simple. Instead of making one type of Zippo case, I made three. When problems arose with the manufacturer I had hurriedly chosen, I was forced to camp out on the floor of his workshop so I could watch over every move he made. Looking back, it's a wonder we didn't kill each other.

The experience with the Zippo cases taught me the importance of one of Cano's favorite expressions—KISS, meaning Keep It Simple, Stupid. When one is starting off on a new venture, it's tempting to try to be everything to everybody. In reality, success comes most easily by focusing on an initial product or service. The time to get more complex is only after a concept is proven. "Keeping things simple, stupid" is the best way to be smart about doing business in any market.

Be Open to Life-Changing Opportunities

While I was still making Zippo cases, I developed a guitar display cabinet to sell to high-end collectors and Hard Rock Café. In June 1997, Lip Davis, the owner of the company that made my cabinets, invited me to a downtown Nashville Rotary Club luncheon. That invitation changed my life forever.

When Lip and I sat down to eat, I noticed a flyer on the table about an exchange program. It offered young professionals the opportunity to spend six weeks visiting Rotarians in Patagonia, Argentina, and touring their businesses—all expenses paid. After at first thinking it might be too much time to take off from work, too painful to be away from family, and too difficult to learn Spanish, I finally realized it was just too good an opportunity to pass up. My Zippo cases and guitar cabinets could wait.

On my first visit to Argentina in 1998 I didn't even get to Mendoza, but it was an incredible experience nonetheless. The friends I made, the music I danced to, the food I ate, and the wine I drank had a profound psychological influence on me. When I returned home, I dreamed about Argentina every night for weeks and immediately made plans to go back and see more of the country with which I had fallen in love.

Thanks in part to the encouragement of William Sandy, a friend who had spent time in Mendoza on a U.S. State Department exchange program and told me it held great potential, in 1999 I put my licensing business on hold and moved to Mendoza for six months to explore business opportunities. I just *knew* the region was going to take off. But I discovered I was too early. Argentina's currency was still pegged to the U.S. dollar, which meant that the country was too expensive to attract foreign tourists in large numbers. I thought that exporting wine might be a good business, but Mendoza's wines weren't competitively priced with those of similar quality from other parts of the world. I sent samples to Australia, Japan, and the United States, but no one was interested in buying.

I did, however, improve my Spanish, make valuable contacts, and learn a lot about how Argentines live, work, and play. As a result, I was much better prepared to move to and start a business in the country when I eventually decided to become an expatriate entrepreneur.

Looking back, I recall that there were well over a hundred people in attendance at the Rotary Club luncheon that day in 1997; yet, almost no one applied for the exchange program with Argentina.

The fact is, many people are not open to life-changing opportunities. A young accountant who once worked for me turned down an offer to spend a year in Germany, all expenses paid, because she felt she would miss her parents. In an ever more competitive global marketplace, her lack of international experience will no doubt limit her future career options. If you truly want to be an entrepreneur in a place like Argentina, you can't afford to make the same mistake. Taking advantage of opportunities for personal and professional growth, whether an exchange program, church mission, semester abroad, or internship overseas, could change your current life into the life of your dreams.

Find a Supportive Friend or Partner

Herman W. Lay, founder of Frito-Lay, got his start in Nashville in the 1930s. As a child, I bought tennis shoes in the building that once housed H.W. Lay Distribution Co. I also bought gasoline across the street from Ed Johnson, who had purchased $8,000 of Lay stock in 1948 as a goodwill gesture toward his friend and fellow entrepreneur. It was a pretty good investment. Fifty years later, the Johnson estate donated $25 million to neighboring Belmont University.

Despite growing up in Nashville, I probably never would have met Herman Lay's son if I hadn't visited Mendoza. By coincidence, shortly after my first trip there, Ward Lay started to think about leveraging his connections in the food and beverage industry to develop a high-end Argentine wine for the U.S. market. Although he owned Estancia Alicura, an 80,000-hectare (200,000-acre) ranch in Patagonia near the town of San Martin de los Andes, Ward hadn't spent much time in Mendoza, where his winery was going to be built. So when a mutual friend put us in touch in 2002, Ward and I began a conversation that has lasted to this day about the trials and tribulations of doing business in Argentina. That conversation, at times held over a glass of Chardonnay in Dallas where Ward lives and at times over a glass of Malbec in Mendoza, was the birth of our friendship as well as my business.

Talking with Ward, I saw that finding a reliable partner in Argentina, keeping contractors on time and on budget, and communicating with the locals were big challenges even for a multimillionaire with a great deal of international business experience. Hearing his stories made me realize that Ward and other foreign investors needed someone on the ground in Mendoza they could trust—someone who could act as a nexus between them and the locals. With Ward's encouragement, I decided to move to Mendoza on a permanent basis in 2003 to start a company to serve that need. English & Associates was born, and Ward Lay was one of my first clients.

The seed of a business often starts to grow far from the place where it is eventually planted. One reason is that friendships based on a common interest can lead to the development of an idea, the discovery of an opportunity, or the formation of a partnership. Seek out others who share your passion, and you just might find not only a great friend but also a future client or partner.

Do as the Romans Do

While my consulting company was getting off the ground in 2003 and 2004, I enrolled in the Executive MBA program at Austral University in Buenos Aires. I had always intended to go back to school to get an advanced degree, and that seemed like the perfect time. The program was one of the top ranked in Latin America and appreciably less expensive than nearly every business school back home. Little did I know that the experience would teach me as much about the importance of language and culture in business as it would about finance and accounting.

I had been educated since kindergarten to raise my hand and wait to be called on before I spoke, but my Argentine peers simply blurted out their comments and questions during class. To my amazement, they were enthusiastically credited for participation, rather than scolded for a lack of manners. I was bewildered when, after a particularly riotous class, the professor scolded *me* for keeping quiet. Talk about culture clash!

Studying with my team members was also a challenge. They insisted on reading entire case studies aloud as a group before discussing them. I didn't understand why each person couldn't read the case and then give his or her individual input to the team. The apparent lack of efficiency drove me crazy, but the experience taught me the value Argentines put on group interaction and consensus.

In addition, because Spanish isn't my native language, I suffered in outdoor team challenges. I'll never forget trying to build a wooden bridge with my classmates within a ten-minute deadline. It was humiliating at thirty-three to be relegated to the sidelines of a project for a lack of communication skills.

At times, I wanted to throw in the towel and quit, but I'm glad I didn't. I learned there are many numbers, charts, acronyms, and graphs to explain how individuals, industries, and companies function. But more important, I learned that when in Rome you really do have to do as the Romans do. No matter how you were educated, if the locals scream and shout to gain attention, you'd better learn to scream and shout as well—even louder than they do and in *their own language*. Adapting is the only way to survive as an entrepreneur in a foreign land.

Bring People Together

As I worked toward my MBA, I learned the value of getting people together to share ideas and solve problems. The experience made me realize that Mendoza's expatriate entrepreneurs could benefit from a little networking. We faced common challenges, yet we barely knew one another and hardly ever interacted. It was time to start a club.

With the support of Carl Emberson, the Fiji-born manager of the Park Hyatt Mendoza, the Mendoza Expats Club was born. In September 2005, about twenty people attended our first luncheon. The next month, nearly seventy came, including my friend Ward Lay (who was kind enough to sponsor our meeting with his new wine, Andeluna). The club was an instant success.

Frenchman Jerome Constant, who owns Anna Bistró restaurant, was also at the very first meeting. "I didn't think there were enough foreigners in town to fill a room," he recalls. "But I was wrong. It was just that no one had taken the initiative to track everyone down and organize a meeting. I was amazed by how many of us there actually were, and how good it felt to get together as a group."

As president of the club, I had the job of getting to know every expatriate entrepreneur, executive, and investor in the city. Eventually, this enabled me to visualize the entire foreign community in my head and understand the relationships between most of the people in it. That knowledge became invaluable to my business and the businesses of my club's members.

When I picked up clients at the airport, I gave them a copy of Charlie O'Malley's *Wine Republic* magazine. If they needed a room, I sent them to Gustavo Espitia's Aguamiel hotel. If they preferred the Hyatt, I called Carl Emberson and arranged for an exclusive rate. If they wanted to visit wineries, I put them in touch with Carolyn Gallagher at Uncorking Argentina. If they were hungry, I sent them to see Jerome Constant at Anna Bistró. And, if customers of Charlie, Gustavo, Carl, Carolyn, or Jerome said they wanted to invest in or start a business in Argentina, I got the call. It was a win-win arrangement.

Of course, the Mendoza Expats Club is about a lot more than business. Should a club member have a bad experience with a local real estate agent, restaurant, hotel, or tour operator, everyone finds out. If someone needs help finding a babysitter, a Spanish tutor, or a reliable accountant, a fellow expat is sure to provide a good recommendation. In short, the club is a rock of stability in an ocean of tall waves.

Most important, starting the club gave me the chance to give back to the people of Mendoza. Along with Monica Pescarmona, head of Grameen Foundation's Mendoza branch, I organized an annual charity ball and art auction to support not only local artists but also entrepreneurs from the city's poorest neighborhoods. In 2008, the renowned American economist Joseph Stiglitz attended our dinner and donated for auction signed copies of his book *Making*

Globalization Work. It was a great honor to meet Stiglitz and secure his support for the betterment of people for whom globalization sometimes doesn't work so well. Back home, I never would have been able to rub shoulders with the likes of Joseph Stiglitz or help disenfranchised people in the developing world become entrepreneurs.

An expats club can be one of the best ways to meet other people who have already done what you are contemplating and learn from their experiences. It's also a great venue for forming personal relationships that can lead to winning business relationships. If a club exists where you are going, join it. If not, form one. Even if it's only you and three others who meet on a regular basis, you'll be amazed at the benefits of bringing people together.

Get Involved in the Community

In 2005, I met the internationally renowned and aptly named conductor David Handel. Born and raised in Buffalo, New York, David spends most of his time outside the United States conducting orchestras in every corner of the world, from Poland to Bolivia to Iraq. In 2005, it just so happened that he was musical director of Mendoza's Cuyo University symphony orchestra. The timing couldn't have been better.

Because Nashville had recently built one of the finest concert halls in the world, and because I had played trumpet in the youth orchestra as a child, I pondered starting a musician exchange with my hometown. Having spent 1989 in Australia on an American Field Service exchange and March 1998 in Argentina on a Rotary exchange, I was convinced of the life-changing power of such programs. Could an exchange between musicians bring Nashville and Mendoza closer together? David Handel and I didn't doubt it for a second.

In May of 2007, David and I escorted four Mendoza musicians to Nashville. They got their share of Southern culture, visiting honky-tonks, eating fried chicken and biscuits, and drinking Jack Daniels whisky. Best of all, the musicians made friends with their peers in Nashville and played with them in two concerts.

In October, four Nashville musicians visited Mendoza. They enjoyed their share of Argentine culture, visiting tango parlors, eating barbecue ribs and blood sausage, and drinking Malbec wine. Better still, the musicians made friends with their peers in Mendoza and continued the practice of sharing the stage in two concerts. It was an exchange program in the purest sense.

About the same time, Philip Rasico, a Vanderbilt University professor of Spanish and Catalan languages, was trying to get Mendoza to sign a sister city agreement with Nashville. He wasn't having much luck. Despite Phil's making several trips to Mendoza and attending several meetings with politicians, the people in Mendoza just didn't get what all the fuss was about. Phil needed help.

Because I was from Nashville but living in Mendoza, I could act as the local coordinator for the sister city initiative. Having someone on the ground broke the logjam. I picked up the phone, called the city's new mayor, Victor Fayad, and immediately set up a meeting. To his credit, "Viti" understood the proposal and supported it. In March 2009, Nashville's mayor, Karl Dean, visited Mendoza and signed the agreement making Nashville and Mendoza sister cities. In September of 2010, I took Mayor Fayad with me to Nashville, where we spent several days shadowing Mayor Dean, visiting local universities, and meeting with business leaders. It had always been my goal to bring together the two places I most love in the world. Now it was a reality.

The musician exchange and the sister city initiative both gave me the opportunity to do something positive for the community in which I live. In doing so, I formed valuable relationships with key people in Mendoza as well as leaders back home. Ironically, I probably never would have met the mayor of Nashville if I hadn't been living in Mendoza.

Being an expatriate entrepreneur in an emerging market is about a lot more than running a business. It's also about playing an active role in the community and looking for opportunities to be a positive influence. If you draw on the same creativity you used to start your company, you can do a world of good for the arts and education.

In the process, you may discover that you have not only helped others but also helped yourself to grow personally and professionally.

Conclusion
You Can't Soar if You Don't Fly

Opportunities to "defy fortune's spite" and overcome circumstances seemingly beyond our control are hidden all around us in jobs for which we are "unqualified," last-minute trips overseas, surprise business proposals, unexpected learning experiences, accidental friendships, and even adversity. As Einstein said, "In the middle of difficulty lies opportunity." If you want the opportunity to be an entrepreneur in an emerging market, you must embrace the challenges, hardships, and trials by fire that are an inherent part of the journey.

Your endeavor will thrive or perish based on *who you are*. Your education, your culture, and your experiences are the golden assets that make you unique and competitive. When you're properly motivated, there are no limits to what you can accomplish in a developing country like Argentina.

LESSON 1

Hidden in the flames of adversity and the ashes of destruction that come from change on a global scale are the opportunities to fly away and begin anew in an emerging market.

2

The Lucky Irishman

CHARLIE'S STORY

"I was in the right place at the right time."
—CHARLIE O'MALLEY

Charlie O'Malley is a redheaded Irishman in his late thirties who exudes the charm and good nature for which his countrymen are famous. You could say that being an expatriate is in his blood; all of his grandfather's fourteen brothers and sisters immigrated to New York City in the early twentieth century, where the O'Malley name is now the stuff of legend.

Today, Charlie's *Wine Republic* magazine is a glossy bimonthly publication read by locals and tourists alike. Even the language schools use it as a teaching aid, and the Mendocinos love it because it helps them improve their English reading skills. As a result, ad revenues, profits, and Charlie's prestige have flourished. So have his other businesses.

"In the beginning, the magazine was like a school project. It was quite amateur. But it was the seed of everything else," Charlie says, referring to his later success as a writer for Frommer's guidebooks, a journalist for *Time Out* and *National Geographic Traveler* magazines, and owner of Trout & Wine, a sightseeing company that gives English-only wine tours.

In keeping with his Irish heritage, Charlie modestly attributes his success in publishing and tourism to "luck." He is adamant that

33

good timing had a lot to do with his good fortune. "I have to stress the main reason for my success has been the success of Mendoza," he says. However, when you read Charlie's story, you will realize that he positioned himself to be lucky and "doubled down" on his bets when he was doing well. His success wasn't by chance.

Charlie is a writer by profession. In Ireland and England he wrote short stories, plays, radio shows, and even a film, but he dreamed in vain of seeing a book published with his name on the cover and the stable income to go along with it. "I was tired and ready for a change, fascinated by Latin America, and looking for a business opportunity." So, in September 2001, Charlie boarded a plane for South America, in search of a new life full of "color and chaos."

"In Ireland, I wrote three or four hours a day, but I became frustrated and stopped," he says. "In Colombia and Ecuador, I found that I could make a living teaching English, and ironically that made me fall back in love with the language. I started writing again. It's a bit of a cliché, but when you travel, you do indeed go on an inner journey and rediscover yourself. Just going to a new culture was invigorating for me."

With a renewed passion for his profession, Charlie kept his eyes open for business opportunities as he traveled South America for a year and a half. "I did find opportunities in Colombia and Venezuela, but the problem was that they were in Colombia and Venezuela. Back then, if you put a suit on in Colombia, you'd get kidnapped." Still, Charlie admired the raw entrepreneurial spirit he witnessed during his travels: "I'll never forget the guy I saw on the street in Caracas, Venezuela, who had jerry-rigged an old home telephone to an overhead line running into a government office building. He was renting it out to passers-by for ten cents a call. You just don't get that kind of creativity back in cold, gray Europe."

As luck would have it, Charlie arrived in Mendoza in January of 2003. Why Mendoza? "I had always been interested in wine yet never could afford it. You need loads of cash to be a wine buff in Europe. Here, you could get the best wines for twenty or thirty

THE LUCKY IRISHMAN: CHARLIE'S STORY

pesos [then equivalent to seven to ten U.S. dollars]." Climate was also a big draw. "From an Irishman's point of view, you can't exaggerate how good the weather is here," says Charlie. "Not having to worry about clouds and wind is wonderful. Now I think of rain as exotic!"

In addition to, and partly because of, great wine and great climate, Charlie saw business potential. "I was here for the famous Vendimia wine festival and couldn't find any information about it in English. Every tourist city I had visited on my trip, even little Iquitos in the Peruvian jungle, had its free English rag. In Mendoza, there was nothing online and nothing even at the city tourism office. I couldn't believe that such a beautiful place with such a huge potential for English-language tourism had no English publications and no English-speaking tour companies. After two days in town, I said, 'I'm staying. This is too good an opportunity to pass up.'"

Let's take a closer look at Charlie's story to find out just why it is that distant pastures sometimes really are greener.

Just Do It

When my brother and I were growing up in Nashville, we often got together with friends to play basketball. Steven, who had never played on an organized team, infuriated our friends, not because he nearly always beat them but because he did so with such an incredible lack of form. His game was so ugly that a stunned onlooker once commented, "I've never seen a guy with absolutely no coordination play basketball so well."

Of course, what our friends didn't realize was that Steven's athletic talent was innate. Even if it was unpolished, it was within him and just as valid as their developed ability. That's the thing about people with certain "built-in" skills: they can be successful if they just show up for the game, get on the court, and make a shot. After all, they might just get lucky, and the ball might just go in.

Charlie O'Malley's success is due in part to the fact that he has the same "just get in the game" philosophy my brother had.

"My interns always ask me about how to break into writing and journalism. I can only tell them my own experience: Just get it out there. Publish something yourself if you have to. It doesn't matter what it looks like, as long as you get it in print," he insists. "When I started the magazine, it was black and white. We made copies on an ancient Xerox machine. But, you know what? Several editions later, the Frommer's writer for Argentina was in Mendoza. The girl at the reception desk in his hotel hands him the magazine, he gives me a call, we go for a beer, and within a year I'm writing for Frommer's—not just for Argentina but also for Uruguay, Paraguay, and Central America. So, now I actually have books [I authored] on the shelf, a dream I always had. It was purely because I started the magazine, rather than sending out manuscripts or CDs to publishers. Do it yourself, get the word out there, and people will pick up on it."

Like people who won't try to speak a foreign language for fear they won't utter the perfect sentence, those who hesitate to act because they are waiting for the perfect moment or the perfect product either never learn, never get in the game, or end up with the greatest product never launched. Charlie is quick to admit that he speaks Spanish with a horrible Irish accent, but by force of will he opens his mouth and makes himself understood. He has no illusions about being perfect and no qualms about at times being a little "sloppy." Charlie is so successful now that he has to turn down opportunities that only a few years ago he would have given almost anything to have. "Frommer's asked me to write a coffee table book on Ireland, but I had to refuse because of my obligations here in Mendoza. I have an intense tour business now, and I can't afford to go anywhere in the high season."

As you are contemplating your own emerging market venture, remember that innate talent is more important than perfection. Whatever the game is that you're good at, take the ball and run with it. You might just get lucky and end up with a slam dunk.

Build on Your Success

Publishing a magazine wasn't the end of the story for Charlie O'Malley. Like any good Irishman enjoying a streak of good luck, he increased his bets by expanding into wine tourism. How? "By accident," he says, in typical self-effacing fashion. "A lot of people make a big deal out of business plans and business projections. I'm not saying they're unnecessary, but from my personal experience, success comes from testing different things."

In the early days, Charlie didn't think his magazine was going to make money on its own, so he experimented with other projects. "The magazine gave me a vehicle to try new businesses such as translation services, accommodations, and wine tours," he recalls. "If one thing didn't work, I'd quickly try another one and another one. It was never, 'Let's try this for two years to see what happens.'"

Once, Charlie sent promotional flyers to travel agencies all over the world. He never heard back from any of them. However, because of the magazine and its website, he did get e-mails from "Stan and his girlfriend in New York" asking about one-day wine tours in English. "People came to us directly, and we didn't expect that," Charlie remembers. "Through trial and error, we realized we had another business on our hands."

As to why he is successful in tourism, Charlie quips, "Alcohol is a major factor! Wine tours have an immediate advantage because, although people are always in a bad mood when we pick them up at their hotel in the morning, by ten o'clock, they've already had three glasses of wine and are giggling like schoolgirls." In a more serious tone, he adds, "It's a great business to be in because it's about making people happy. I love transferring the passion I feel about Mendoza to people who have just arrived here."

Of course, Charlie made occasional mistakes along the way. One such misstep is the stuff of legend in the local expat community. "I was guiding two Orthodox Jews on a wine tour and thought it would be a great idea to take them to lunch at Mendoza's famous Posada del Jamón [House of Ham]. Not until we were sitting down to eat and looking at the menu did I find out they didn't eat pork. In the end, I got the restaurant to serve them salad and cheese, and I had all the ham! That day I learned that in tourism you can't always be yourself. You have to know your customers and adapt to their needs."

Bad restaurant choices aside, Charlie's story shows us how an initial success can be the foundation for expanding an existing business or starting a new one. In his case, he used a low-cost method of trial and error by advertising ideas for services in his magazine in order to identify the most promising opportunities. Then, he got going despite being a little rough around the edges. By leveraging his passion for and knowledge about Mendoza, he was able to quickly build a new business that complemented the magazine. Once you have established yourself as an entrepreneur in an emerging market and are enjoying a certain degree of success, don't miss the chance to double down on your bets as Charlie did.

Start Small and Keep Costs Down

Like many expatriate entrepreneurs in Mendoza, Charlie found Argentina's low-cost operating environment a big help. "If I were starting a magazine back in Ireland or England, I'd probably need ten investors. I'd need a board of directors. I'd have to get their agreement on every business decision. However, that's not the case here. After the 2001 crisis in Argentina, you could start a business for nothing. The first edition of the magazine cost me AR$1,000 (then about US$330). The monthly rent on my first office was AR$400 (then about US$130). I would have come here anyway, but the low cost was a draw."

Charlie emphasizes the importance of starting small and growing with the business instead of ahead of it. "If we had started with a big glossy magazine, we would've been out of business in six months," he says.

For the first year, Charlie published the magazine out of his house. Only after the publication and the wine tours were proven successes did he rent a small two-office space above a travel agency. Charlie's office had noisy and often broken air conditioners, 1960s-era furniture, and a rickety old staircase. But it also had a big red sign on the door advertising his tours in English. Charlie explains, "As a foreigner here, foreign tourists and locals alike trust you. I can't express how much of an advantage it is to speak English fluently. Putting an English sign on your door attracts customers more than anything else."

Initially, Charlie spent money only on what mattered most to building his business and ignored the fancy frills. He realized that English-speaking tourists cared about English-speaking tour guides, not broken air conditioners. Charlie invested his funds accordingly and, after six years of sacrifice, moved into beautiful new offices in October 2009. With the wind at his back, he even splurged on custom-built furniture.

Avoid the temptation to overdo it when embarking on your emerging market enterprise. Starting small and keeping costs down is often the secret to long-term success.

Adapt to the Local Environment

In the 1960s, psychologists measured how much time drivers in different regions of the United States waited behind a car stopped at a green traffic light before they honked their horns. Northerners honked almost immediately when the light turned green. In the South, many drivers never honked, even if a car sat through the entire green light without moving. In short, certain aspects of culture are manifested in the driving habits of a people.

In Mendoza, some drivers don't wait for the green light to get going. They also run through intersections on yellow and even recently turned red lights. You would think that as a result there would be a lot of accidents at intersections, but that's not the case. Because of unwritten rules, or culture, those who "jump the gun" on green know to make sure crossing traffic is actually stopping rather than accelerating to beat a changing light. The same is true with respect to right of way. Streets of high importance do not yield to anyone. But who knows what streets are considered important? Only the locals. Want to drive successfully in Mendoza? You'd better learn the rules that aren't printed in the driver's education handbook, no matter how illogical or illegal they may seem to you based on your culture back home.

Expatriate entrepreneurs' ability to play by the local rules of the game is demonstrated not only in their "reformed" driving habits but also in the way they do business. Charlie O'Malley offers us an example of dealing with the infamous Argentine bureaucracy.

"Bureaucracy is a cultural issue. You have to change your attitude to deal with it successfully. You have to go with the flow and not let things eat at you. I both ignore it and follow it," Charlie explains. For the first three years, he wasn't registered as a tourism agency, but he operated anyway. "I just paid someone else for his registration number and put it on the sign. In a developing country, you learn to dance around the bureaucracy in your initial years, and then eventually you find solutions." Charlie says it's important to accept bureaucracy for what it is and adapt. "If you hate queuing for three hours at the bank or the tax office, just find someone else to do it!"

Entrepreneurs from around the world who successfully start businesses in emerging markets like Argentina are able to do so in part because they adapt to the local culture. Not adapting is like trying to play Monopoly with three people who have a different set of rules than yours. You can insist all you want that your rules are better or fairer, but if you don't play by their rules, you will lose every time.

Ride the Waves of Change

Charlie O'Malley is an example of how success can be found or further developed by taking advantage of industry changes in an emerging market. In 2004, it was obvious that many more English-speaking tourists would be coming to Mendoza, yet most local wineries and tour operators didn't have the knowledge, the desire, or the right attitude to serve them. Charlie explains, "I moved to a place where it was very hard [for a tourist] to do a winery tour in English. You needed help, especially if you were short on time. I saw that the locals either weren't able or weren't willing to serve the needs of English-speaking tourists, and I decided to fill the gap." Despite the huge increase in these tourists visiting Mendoza, many local operators *still* haven't repositioned themselves to take advantage of the boom. Most of Charlie's competition comes from other foreign-owned tour companies.

Charlie also recognized and embraced the trends in technology that are radically changing the worldwide industry. "There's been a fundamental shift in tourism in the past decade because of the Internet. It has literally opened up the world to me as a tour operator. There must be ten sites I log onto every day to run my business."

As a local operator, Charlie now has much more advance contact with a customer who will eventually take one of his tours. Before, a person who lived in New York would call a New York–based travel agent, who then called or faxed a tour operator overseas to arrange the details. Today, Charlie reaches people directly through Google ads and two websites, which he makes more visible via Twitter and Facebook. "Being tech-savvy is key," he says.

Nonetheless, technology can also be a double-edged sword. Charlie says that thanks to the Internet, potential customers are more informed than ever. "If I don't step up and perform at my best, there are serious repercussions, like nasty comments on the Web. If people complain at the end of a tour, I do *not* dismiss them. I give them a refund. I am *super* nice to them. Sites like TripAdvisor are half tyrannical in a sense. They can be my best friend or my worst nightmare."

Technology that makes payment easy on an international scale is another critical enabler for Charlie's business. "PayPal is a major tool. A customer pays me in the States, the money goes into my account in England within five minutes, and I provide the service in Argentina two months later. There's no other way I could get tourists to pay in advance when they don't know me."

Charlie explains the difference between doing business in the tourism industry now and ten years ago: "There was more room for error, so people were accustomed to not getting exactly what they expected. Now, customers' expectations are higher and they are becoming more demanding. Tourism is no longer that faceless guy talking on a microphone to a busload of forty people. Now it's more personal. People want that face-to-face experience throughout the transaction. Technology enables that."

As the old saying goes, the only certainty in life is change. In emerging markets where substantial change is likely due to burgeoning industries or socioeconomic factors, opportunities abound for expatriate entrepreneurs like Charlie O'Malley. Be on the lookout for places where one or more sectors have the potential for rapid growth, and position yourself to serve them. Leveraging your unique perspective as an outsider, as well as the latest technology, will very likely give you a competitive advantage.

Conclusion
Who You Are Matters

Luck, in the form of good timing, was certainly on Charlie's side. He insists, "A major factor in my success was that Mendoza was a blank canvas when I arrived. It never had an English-language magazine. Tourism was just taking off. I was in the right place at the right time." Perhaps, but Charlie was also the right *person* at the right time.

The Roman philosopher Seneca said, "Luck is what happens when preparation meets opportunity." I can think of no better example than Charlie O'Malley. Other entrepreneurs also identified and developed opportunities in Mendoza that leveraged their skills, knowledge, and sense of untapped potential. However, no one else published an English-language magazine. They were too busy building some other business based on whatever it was they were already good at, enjoyed, or knew. Charlie was able to seize the day because of his innate writing abilities, his knowledge of successful English publications in other parts of Latin America, and his realization that in Mendoza there was untapped demand for something he was confident that he could do.

When pressed, Charlie admits that even in the area of tourism he actually had previous experience that turned out to be valuable. "When I was nineteen, I lived in Paris for a year, and I worked for a travel agency that took busloads of French kids back to Ireland on exchange programs. It was a summer job and I loved it. So tourism came naturally to me." In fact, in both of his ventures Charlie took relevant experience from his previous life and applied it to his new one.

If someone else did consider launching an English-language magazine in 2003, or doing English wine tours in 2004, he or she didn't have the background, skills, or "just-get-it-out-there" determination of Charlie O'Malley. They daydreamed and then went home without bothering to spend even a thousand pesos to publish a black-and-white "rag" on an old Xerox copier . . . and were never heard from again.

LESSON 2

Luck, in the form of good timing, is important to building a business in an emerging market. Having the experience to recognize good timing and the skills to take advantage of it are even more important.

3

Birds of a Feather

"From the beginning, I had a great partner in Pablo.
None of this would be possible without him."
—MICHAEL EVANS

When I first visited the offices and tasting room of The Vines of Mendoza, I said to myself, "These guys are *crazy*." I had met Michael Evans in a café only a few months before. At that time, he was batting around various business ideas and wanted to know what I thought about them.

Now it was February of 2006. Michael, his business partners, Pablo Giménez Riili and David Garrett (who left the company in 2008 to start another venture), and I were standing in the middle of a dilapidated house, surrounded by frantic construction workers. Dust and dirt were everywhere. Even worse, it was only one month before the annual Vendimia harvest festival, the biggest event of the year in Mendoza. If the offices and tasting room weren't finished by then, the fledgling company would miss the peak tourist season and *it* would be finished.

Above the scream of a handsaw Michael confidently shouted, "We'll be done in twenty days!" *Buena suerte*, I thought. Good luck!

Thanks to his blond hair and boyish good looks, you could take Michael Evans for a thirty-year-old surfer turned San Jose techie.

45

That would be a mistake. Michael is in his midforties, and starting new businesses has been his passion from a very young age.

A self-confessed workaholic, Michael says he receives 300 e-mails a day and sends out about 150. "In some ways, I'm successful because I work harder than anybody else does," he notes. Ironically, Michael moved to Argentina for a change of lifestyle. "I was thinking that this could be a place to slow down a little bit or at least take a break. It didn't turn out that way! It's been over five years of working six and a half days a week."

It all began in 1986. While Michael was working at a car dealership near Washington, D.C., where he was born and raised, he saw that people needed help to negotiate the price of a used automobile. So he drove out to Phoenix (because *Fortune* magazine ranked the city number one for startups) and launched a company to do just that. "I have always been an entrepreneur," he explains.

Growing up in the nation's capitol, Michael has also always been heavily involved in politics. He worked on every Democratic Party presidential campaign from Bill Clinton in 1992 through John Kerry in 2004.

Michael says that both experiences were key to getting The Vines of Mendoza off the ground. "When I started my first business in Arizona, I was by myself and doing everything from marketing to accounting. In politics, I learned the importance of hard deadlines. After all, election day isn't a date you can just push back."

After Kerry's unsuccessful 2004 campaign, Michael came to Argentina for what he thought was going to be a short vacation from life back home. "If a week before my trip somebody had said I'd end up staying here for five years, I would have told them they were nuts," he recalls.

However, once Michael arrived in Mendoza, he couldn't leave. "I came here expecting a consumer-friendly experience like I had in Napa, Italy, and France, but I couldn't find it anywhere. Argentina felt like a new frontier."

What Michael did find in Mendoza was a new friend and future business partner. At the suggestion of a woman he met at a wine-tasting class in Buenos Aires, when he arrived in Mendoza, Michael called Pablo Giménez Riili. "I expected Pablo to meet with me for a quick cup of coffee, but he took two days off from work to show me around town. He even invited me to an *asado* at his family's house and introduced me to Fernet [an Italian liquor that Argentines drink with Coca-Cola]. We hit it off instantly and have been like brothers ever since."

Michael decided to stay in Mendoza for six months, do some research, and write a business plan with Pablo. The premise was, "Given that Mendoza is going to grow into a great wine destination, what kinds of goods and services will be needed?"

Michael and Pablo proposed starting a small hotel, wine-tasting room, and direct wine sales business. "We developed these concepts to solve the problems I had as a consumer. If somebody had started this business before we did, I would have been a big customer," Michael explains.

So it is that five years after thinking *"Buena suerte,"* I find myself visiting Michael Evans again at the corporate offices and tasting room of The Vines of Mendoza. The dust has long since settled. I'm now standing in the reception area of what is perhaps the most high-profile and successful foreign-owned venture in Mendoza, of which Michael is cofounder and CEO.

"In addition to our original tasting room and online shop, we run a wine store in the Park Hyatt Mendoza, manage over eighty privately owned vineyard estates in Valle de Uco, have a direct wine sales business back in the States, make wine in our recently completed winery, and will break ground on a resort by the end of the year," he tells me. Michael, Pablo, and their company have done so well that they have been featured in major media including *Bloomberg, BusinessWeek, Financial Times, Fodor's, Food & Wine, Forbes, Investors Business Daily, Newsweek, Vanity Fair, The New York Times, The Wall Street Journal, The Washington Post,* and *Wine Enthusiast.*

Read on to discover how Michael Evans went from car dealerships and Democrats to vines and wines.

Solve a Problem

Michael Evans wanted to try as many wines as possible. He had traveled eight thousand miles to Mendoza, and, like many tourists, he didn't think he would return. However, it took an hour to get to each winery and then two hours to do a tour and tasting. He arrived with the goal of tasting fifty to seventy-five wines. By the end of his three-day trip, Michael had tasted "perhaps twelve."

So, what did he do? "With Pablo I opened a tasting room where people could try ten, fifteen, or even twenty wines in one place without having to go out to each individual winery." Problem solved.

Michael also knew from personal experience that it was not easy for tourists to carry wine back with them in the airplane and that finding Mendoza wines at home was difficult or impossible. "Argentina is not like France, Italy, or Napa; if you go to those places and try a great wine, you can probably find it where you live." So he started taking orders for wine in the tasting room and shipping it directly to customers in the United States from a twenty-thousand-bottle warehouse in Napa.

People who successfully start businesses outside their home countries are generally good at identifying solutions to problems or needs they have experienced. Especially in developing nations, this can be relatively easy to do. When tourists complain of a lack of infrastructure, bad service in hotels and restaurants, and no one who speaks their language, expatriate entrepreneurs hear the call of opportunity loud and clear. Michael Evans built the first tasting room in Mendoza, and five years later it is *still* the only one of its kind in town. His story is proof that by coming up with a solution to a problem, you can create a business in an emerging market.

Be Ready to Expand

Michael had a bold vision for a company based in Mendoza, and because of its proposed scale he knew he would have to find additional capital. "I started with my savings, then credit card debt, then family and close friends; but that only got us to about US$200,000," he remembers. So Michael began reaching out to friends of friends. "We never got any money from venture capital firms. It was all friends or angel investors." Ironically, Michael's fund-raising strategy led to the business that has become the foundation of his success.

When Michael initially went to raise money, the three pillars of the business plan were direct wine sales, a tasting room, and a resort hotel. However, an additional concept quickly emerged. Many friends who were also potential investors said they were interested in the project but wanted to own a small vineyard next to the resort. At the same time, Michael was looking for land to plant his own vineyard and discovering that if he didn't have a well, tractor, and other equipment, "a ten-acre, $200,000 vineyard was suddenly going to cost me a million dollars." Michael realized that he needed to expand his initial concept: "I said, 'Let's look at this venture as a resort with a vineyard cooperative and get a bunch of people together to make it happen.'"

Michael's original idea was a project for ten friends with ten acres each. However, it turned out that so many foreign tourists and investors had the dream to have their own vineyard in Argentina that the project grew substantially. In fact, The Vines of Mendoza's largest business by far is vineyard development and management. "Now we've got over a thousand acres of vineyard estates," Michael explains. "It is 80 percent of what we do."

He expanded his business model even further in 2008 when an opportunity arose to create a wine bar in the prestigious Park Hyatt Mendoza just across the street from The Vines of Mendoza's existing tasting room. "If you think about the one place where our target market for vineyard estates is most concentrated, it would be the Hyatt hotel with its 187 rooms. That's our sweet spot," he says.

Michael had in fact been talking to the hotel for years, but it wasn't until the management decided to build a new restaurant that his vision became possible. "They were going to be remodeling anyway, so they asked for proposals," Michael remembers. "We went through a very competitive bidding process." In the end, The Vines of Mendoza won the bid and made a significant investment in the wine bar. "It's been a great success," Michael says. "Several people who first got to know about us at our location in the Hyatt later purchased lots in our vineyard development. Our presence at the hotel has really helped to strengthen the Vines of Mendoza brand."

Michael's story demonstrates the importance of expanding on an initial concept if demand calls for it or if a unique opportunity presents itself. By listening to feedback from friends and incorporating it into his plans, he not only secured the funding he needed but also ensured the future success of his business. And by expanding operations into the very heart of his target market, Michael developed a direct-sales channel at Mendoza's most prestigious hotel that his late-arriving competitors now find impossible to duplicate. As you are launching your emerging market company, be flexible and look for opportunities to change your plans in a positive way. Remember: 80 percent of Michael's current business has nothing to do with his original concept!

Find a Partner Who Believes "Impossible Is Nothing"

Pablo Giménez Riili comes from a large, well-known family with a tradition of wine making going back to 1945. In that year, his grandfather moved to Mendoza. Don Pedro Gimenez would surely be impressed with the partnership between his grandson and Michael Evans. In fact, the description of the Gimenez Riili company on the family's website, "a combination of innovation and character with a promising future," could apply to Pablo and Michael's relationship as well.

Pablo is in his late thirties, thin, and unusually tall for an Argentine. He stands out at social and business gatherings, not only because of his physical stature but also because of the *buena onda* (good vibes) he radiates with his positive and outgoing personality—just like Michael. It's no wonder they get along so well. They are birds of a feather.

Michael and Pablo's relationship is exemplified in the phrase, "Impossible is nothing." This twist on the old saying was coined by

Pablo when he and Michael began the tasting room project. It has since become the unofficial motto of their company.

"Our clients are bankers, doctors, and lawyers who come from countries where a fast pace and top-quality service are expected," Michael says. A sign with the message "Impossible Is Nothing" hangs over the door between The Vines of Mendoza's back office and the public tasting room. "Every time employees step into the world of our customers, they are reminded that bridging a cultural gap to deliver an amazing product is critical to our success."

It's also a frame of mind that explains how Michael and Pablo overcome seemingly impossible challenges, like building a tasting room in thirty days or a winery in only ninety. How do Michael and Pablo get their staff to go the extra mile? By asking for the impossible, leading by example, and doing whatever it takes to show that the effort is appreciated. Michael says, "When we were building the winery, every day we brought in croissants in the morning and lunch in the afternoon so the workers didn't need to leave to eat. We would cook *asados* for them as well. They'd been working at other places for twenty years and were never treated that way." But having Pablo on board was just as important. According to Michael, "It was a combination of Pablo's know-how and contacts. Because of him, we were able to get contractors to come in and work harder than they normally would, since they already had a relationship with him through the real estate projects he developed."

Building a business is never easy, but it is even less so in an emerging market where a sense of urgency is hardly the norm. However, with a positive attitude and a local partner who can translate expectations into a language everyone can understand, nothing is impossible.

Look Before You Leap

Doing business in emerging markets can be a tremendous challenge for expatriate entrepreneurs, and not just because of differences in language. Even though Michael's Spanish is good and Pablo's

English is excellent, they sometimes have misunderstandings. "Two feet deep" is what they say to remind themselves that it's dangerous to assume anything in a foreign environment.

That slogan emerged from an imaginary scenario they concocted together. It starts with Michael and Pablo standing near the edge of a swimming pool. It's a hot Mendoza night, and Michael is desperate to cool off. He asks his friend, "Is there water in the pool?" Pablo enthusiastically responds, "Yes!" Michael jumps in headfirst, realizing too late that the water is only two feet deep.

Nursing his bruised head, Michael angrily shouts at Pablo, "Why didn't you tell me it was only two feet deep?" Pablo shrugs his shoulders and then shouts back, "You asked if there was water, not how deep it is!"

This imaginary situation demonstrates that culture-based assumptions can lead people to make grave errors in judgment. If Michael had been in Pablo's place, he probably would have thought to say, "There's water in the pool, but be careful because it's very shallow." However, Argentines assume that you know what you're getting into and that if you don't look first, you're an idiot for not checking or not asking.

To make matters worse, people from many cultures nod or say "Yes!" even when they don't understand or agree with something. Michael gives us a good example. "You ask, 'Can you make sure this package is delivered by Friday at 3:00 P.M.?' The response is, 'Yeah, yeah, no problem!' When it finally gets there the following Tuesday, you're left scratching your head and saying, 'What?' Out of embarrassment, people often won't tell you they don't understand."

To avoid the business equivalent of a broken neck from diving into shallow water, look before you leap. It's "buyer beware" in emerging markets like Argentina, whether clearly stated or not. It's *your* responsibility to discover the shortcomings of a potential partner or the problems with a seemingly attractive investment. The other party may not feel obligated or even think to point them out. "Double- and triple-check everything," says Michael. After all, the water might be only two feet deep.

Invest in Experts

When Michael first arrived in Mendoza, he went to see a real estate agent about buying a vineyard. Fortunately, he took a local expert along with him. "The agent didn't realize my attorney could see his computer screen. He was actually taking the time to double the price of each property before printing it out! If I hadn't hired someone to be there with me, I never would have realized."

Bill Gates attributes his success in part to hiring people who are smarter than he is. Michael Evans shares that philosophy. "Contrary to a lot of entrepreneurs I know back home, I'm happy *not* to be the smartest person in the room. I may want to know how to make wine, but I'm not going to try to figure it out on my own just to save a buck. That's a recipe for disaster. I gladly pay experts for their expertise."

Michael also feels his success is due to "great accountants, great attorneys, and great local partners." Whenever he is asked for advice about starting a business overseas, he says, "To succeed, you must be willing to invest in specialists. Even though lawyers and accountants can sometimes be difficult and you'd prefer not to pay them, you've got to make that investment. They know how to get through the bureaucracy and how to make business possible in a foreign environment."

The Argentines have a great saying: "That which is cheap ends up costing a fortune." Nothing could be truer when it comes to cutting corners on the experts. After all, an expatriate entrepreneur in a developing country is a lot like the proverbial "babe in the woods." As the wolves close in, do you really have the time and the local know-how to do everything yourself? It's best to simply pay someone to provide you with what you need so you can start your business quickly, with a minimum of risk. Trying to do it all on your own could cost you your success.

Remember, It's Chinatown

In the final scene of the film noir classic *Chinatown*, Jack Nicholson's character, Jake, is defeated by "the system." As the murdering child molester he captured is set free, Jake is ordered by the police to walk away and forget it. In Chinatown, the rules of the game are just different.

When insurmountable problems arise, Michael Evans and his team turn to each other and say, "It's Chinatown, Jake." That's how they deal with the battles they can't win in Argentina. "It's just the way things are," Michael concedes. "It's impossible to have lunch in less than an hour. And forget about trying to get business cards in a day. You just can't. No one is going to work on a Sunday. They are all going to be at lunch with the family. Argentines have the right priorities in life, but they do make it hard to get things done sometimes!"

Doing business in a foreign land, you have to know which battles you can win and which ones you shouldn't even try to fight. There is a system in place called culture, and you have to follow its rules if you want to get ahead. Saint Francis of Assisi said, "Lord, grant me the serenity to accept the things I cannot change, the courage to change the things I can, and the wisdom to know the difference." Successful expatriate entrepreneurs find partners, hire consultants, and adapt to the local culture so they are sure to know the difference. As Michael says, "There are so many things here that don't make sense to me. But hey, 'It's Chinatown, Jake.' I have no illusions about it being Bel Air."

Conclusion
A Good Partner Makes All the Difference

Michael and Pablo's story shows us that an expatriate's entrepreneurial spirit and a local's integrity and contacts can be a winning combination. In fact, Michael says he wouldn't even have considered starting The Vines of Mendoza if he hadn't met Pablo. "His English is excellent, he's a lawyer, he has experience as a contractor, and his family has been making wine for fifty years. Most of all, he's one of the best people you will ever meet. He was the partner I knew I needed."

About partnerships, Pablo says, "They're like marriages. It's awfully hard to find a good one because both parties have to genuinely care for each other. It can't be about money or convenience. That's why so many business partnerships fail in general and why ours works exceptionally well." Michael adds, "Our relationship works, first, because there is mutual trust; second, because there is good communication; and third, because we truly get along as friends. We spend so much time together that it would be insufferable if we didn't enjoy each other's company!"

In my experience, Michael and Pablo's partnership unfortunately is the exception to the rule. Professionals who are competent lawyers, doctors, or executives often inexplicably lose their common sense when they are investing overseas, forming partnerships without performing due diligence. In effect, they jump into a marriage without first checking out their bride's reputation around town. I know, because once they realize the magnitude of their mistake, I'm often hired to oversee the "divorce."

Michael Evans has no doubts about the importance of a good partnership to his success. "The main reason I have been able to overcome the challenges of doing business here is that from the beginning I had a great local partner in Pablo. None of this would be possible without him."

LESSON 3

With the right local partner in an emerging market, impossible is nothing. With the wrong one, you'll find yourself lost in Chinatown at night. Choose wisely.

4

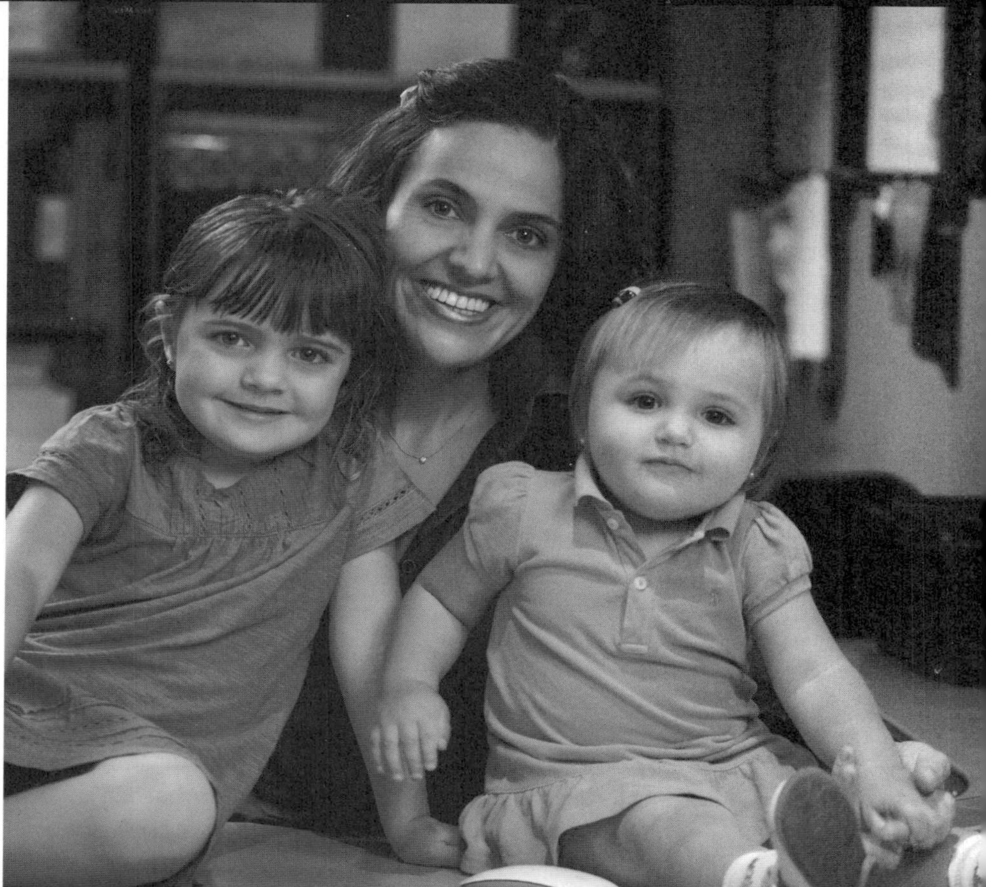

Small and Focused

"You don't need a huge backpack to climb a tall mountain."
—CAROLYN GALLAGHER

Carolyn Gallagher is one of those blue-eyed California girls they write songs about. Her big smile and radiant personality are two of her greatest personal assets, along with her little girls—Carmen, three, and Julia, who is barely ten months old. In fact, while I interviewed Carolyn in her home office, her daughters played happily at our feet. "As you can see, the barrier between the office and the house isn't black and white!" Carolyn told me with a laugh. "There are a lot of family things happening in the office and a lot of business things happening in the house. But, at least we have space and everyone can choose where to work or play."

In addition to running a family, Carolyn owns and operates a high-end tour company called Uncorking Argentina. "My job is to expose the world to all the beautiful things that Mendoza has to offer—the very things that made me fall in love with the region in the first place," she says. Carolyn is obviously doing a good job. Her tours have been praised within the pages of *National Geographic* magazine, and she is now expanding to offer English courses for local professionals who want to improve their wine industry vocabulary. "Uncorking Argentina is like my daughter Carmen. She's a little more grown up, developed, and able. My Wine Language business is more like Julia, in its infancy."

Carolyn was raised in Sacramento, California, where she was an avid white-water rafter and mountain climber. "I was very much an outdoor person," she recalls. She always enjoyed "dreaming up new projects, organizing people, and making things happen," whether as president of her high school class or as a river guide. Not much has changed for her since then. "As an entrepreneur, I work fifteen hours some days, but putting in those fifteen hours is great! I love what I do."

Carolyn's journey to Argentina began in 1990, when Marcela Lledo, an exchange student from Mendoza, spent a year at her high school. "Every day I took Marcela to school in my Mustang convertible, and we shared a locker. Although she didn't live with my family, we became like sisters," Carolyn recalls. The relationship would turn out to be life changing; it was the reason Carolyn visited Argentina for the first time in 1992. "I came to see Marcela and found an undiscovered country. Argentina was vast, it was open, and it had everything I needed. It had great food, great wine, great mountains and rivers, and great people. And Mendoza was a great little city. For me, it was the perfect place to have a family, grow old, and live new experiences. I saw so many opportunities for personal and professional growth that I wanted to come back for good."

Before she made the move to Mendoza, Carolyn attended the University of California at Santa Barbara. There, she played Ultimate Frisbee, sang in a choir, and studied geography and linguistics. "My education prepared me to teach people about the natural and cultural beauty of Mendoza as well as how to get through the language barrier," she says.

After college, Carolyn worked to save money for her move to Argentina. "I was a river guide, a teacher, and a winery worker," she recalls. She even developed a bilingual program for construction companies. "These were jobs to help me make money and be free. I never wanted to be an employee in a large company."

When Carolyn finally left the United States for Mendoza in 1998, it was on a one-way ticket. "I said to myself, 'OK, I'm going on an adventure! I don't know what I'll end up doing, but I'll figure it out.'" After two years of teaching English, Carolyn decided that she wanted to start her own business in Argentina but realized she lacked some key skills. "I needed to go home and take classes, read books, and do research."

Back in California, Carolyn studied cooking, wine making, and business. She also landed a job as a wine rep. According to Carolyn, "I was the unofficial spokesperson in my town for Malbec. It was great fun because I was constantly reading about Argentine wine and teaching people about it. I couldn't wait to race back down to Mendoza and apply what I had learned."

In 2004, Carolyn returned to Argentina with new skills and a new game plan. "I was on the lookout for niches I could fill in wine and education. On one hand, I saw that tourism was taking off, and nobody was doing multifaceted tours that combined outdoor adventure with cooking classes and great wines," Carolyn recalls. "On the other hand, I saw that the locals needed English-language skills to prepare themselves to receive the world." So, Carolyn founded Uncorking Argentina. "The wine tour business was the key to my new life," she says.

In the span of four short years, Carolyn Gallagher married her Argentine boyfriend and gave birth not only to two beautiful children but also to a thriving business far from home. Some might say it was her destiny, since Carolyn's family name comes from *Gallchobhar*, which means "foreign helper" in Irish. However, destiny doesn't entirely explain her success. Let's examine her story to see what she has to teach us about being an expatriate entrepreneur in an emerging market.

Find a Place Where It's Easy to Get Started

One of the reasons Argentina was so appealing to Carolyn was that it was easier to start a small business there than in California. "It requires a lot of preparation to launch a company back home," she says. "I didn't have much money to begin with, so my only option was to put in a lot of hours and to tinker here and there. In the States, you don't exist if that's your strategy. You have to have connections, tons of relevant experience, and an A-to-Z business plan just so you can razzle-dazzle potential investors in the hope of obtaining start-up capital. Here in Argentina, your dollars or euros go a lot further; so from a financial standpoint, it's easier to get started on your own. You just take the leap and go for it, like everyone else in this country does."

Thanks to favorable exchange rates and an entrepreneurial local culture, in some ways it's less complicated to hang out a shingle and start operating in places like Argentina. Carolyn explains, "You don't have to push and shove so much on the front end just so you can suddenly burst onto the scene with a lot of pomp and circumstance and say, 'Here I am!' In the developing world, small businesses have a more natural development curve."

In fact, the percentage of self-made men and women in many emerging markets is higher than in the developed world. Out of sheer economic necessity, it's common for people to start businesses out of their homes, making do with whatever resources they have. The tiny convenience stores called *kioskos* I pass by every evening on my walk home from work are a good example. Despite being located in the garages of private homes, the *kioskos* are professional operations that feature shiny tile floors, bright lighting, vending machines, and counter space. In a nation where garage-based businesses are the norm, neither other people's money nor the perfect business plan is necessary to get your project off the ground. "I'm like the locals," Carolyn says. "Streamlined, flexible, and independent. Here, you don't need a huge backpack to climb a tall mountain."

Be Observant

According to Carolyn, one of the best ways to learn how to do business in a foreign country is to watch how people behave. "I don't think I said more than five words during my first two years in Mendoza!" she jokes. "I just listened and followed."

In particular, Carolyn hung out at one of the city's most popular athletic apparel stores. It was owned by the father of her old high school friend, Marcela Lledo. "I loved watching Marcela's dad do business. I was like a fly on the wall observing every movement and every expression he made," Carolyn remembers. It was in the store that she saw how an Argentine business owner negotiates with vendors, interacts with customers, manages employees, and sets prices. "I was fascinated by the cultural and linguistic aspects of the business. I wanted to participate in that world. I wanted to play in that game."

Carolyn also learned a lot about business from fellow entrepreneur Michael Evans (see Chapter 3). He hired her to teach visitors to his tasting room about the local wine industry and Mendoza culture. "I had always been a one-woman show, a sole proprietor. So it was great to watch Michael and see how he motivated his team by setting goals. Because I had never worked in a large company, The Vines of Mendoza was like a foreign culture to me—very professional and fast paced. If you missed a day there, you missed a year!"

Carolyn emphasizes that observing culture is not simply a form of entertainment: "You can't be a mere spectator of what's going on around you in your new home. You must seek to understand why people act the way they do. You have to take the country's history into consideration. That's the only way to gain a true appreciation for a culture and learn how to successfully operate within it."

Indeed, many foreigners fail at starting a business in an emerging market because they never come to fully understand and respect cultural differences. Instead of trying to figure out what makes the locals tick and adapt to their way of doing things, unsuccessful expatriate entrepreneurs believe they have nothing to learn and everything to teach. That might be true in some areas, such as providing top-quality service to clients from the developed world. However, a condescending attitude makes it difficult if not impossible to interact with employees and service providers. Taking the time to observe how the locals operate and understanding the reasons for their behavior are keys to the adaptation process and the success of any venture. As Carolyn says, "If you want to succeed, you have to stop looking at your watch and start looking at the people."

Reset Your Expectations

When Carolyn arrived in Mendoza in 2004, she thought it would take forever to get her business up and running. "My biggest challenge was in understanding the time line down here," she remembers. "Everything from opening a bank account to setting up an Internet connection seemed incredibly slow and complicated." Nonetheless, she didn't let go of her dream. "I said to myself, 'I'm going to get there one step at a time.'"

While speed often equals success in the developed world, Carolyn believes that the best way to be effective in a country like Argentina is to move slowly yet steadily toward your objective. "Here there's a conviction that solutions to problems arise naturally. If you try to push people too hard they will just look at you like you're crazy." A slower pace can also be more enjoyable. "In the U.S., I felt like I was in a rat race," she recalls. "Here, you close the door to your business at 1:00 P.M. and leave to have lunch with your family. It's refreshing to return to the kind of lifestyle we had back home forty years ago."

"Just relax, and eventually it will all come together," Carolyn advises. "You can't force people to adapt to your schedule." Indeed, entrepreneurs from other cultures often have to accept that it's just not possible to do a hundred things in a twenty-four-hour period. "With luck, you might get five things accomplished. So, you have to say to yourself, 'I got five things done today. That's great!'"

Of course, even after adapting to the pace of the local culture, expatriate entrepreneurs still need clear objectives and well-thought-out plans for how to reach them. "I move slowly, but I carefully plan my steps," notes Carolyn. Moving slowly because of external factors beyond one's control or because of family commitments doesn't mean putting in a couple of hours a day and calling it quits. Carolyn often works seven days a week, hosting wine tours, teaching classes, and answering e-mails—in some cases, with her girls playing on her lap or under her desk. In short, resetting expectations about how long it takes to install a phone line doesn't mean changing the personal work ethic that makes her competitive.

Define Your Objectives and Stay Focused

After she observed how things were done in Argentina and reset her expectations, Carolyn carefully defined objectives for herself and her business. "I decided to stay small and focused. I didn't want to oversell or overcommit." So she set up Uncorking Argentina as a home-based company with only a couple of employees. "I never considered a brick-and-mortar office. My website and my persona are my marketing tools," she states.

I know from personal experience that Carolyn is disciplined about saying no to opportunities that might shift her focus away from her priorities. In 2008, she politely turned down my suggestion that she become president of the Mendoza Expats Club. At the time, I was surprised by her response because she seemed perfect for the job. Now that I know her mission is to work in a sound, professional way and take the time to enjoy what she does, I better understand why she said no. "Since I'm small, I can admire the view and take pleasure in the journey itself. To me, that's what life is all about," she explains.

Carolyn is careful not to overextend herself because the one-on-one relationships she builds with her clients are essential to the success of Uncorking Argentina. She feels that if she grows she will lose the personal touch that makes her business unique. In fact, the interaction with clients is one of the things Carolyn likes most about what she does. "It's not that I simply plan a trip for someone. I help them plan an escape from their reality. I love to baby my clients and make them feel special. I couldn't do that if I were sitting in an office managing employees."

In places like Argentina, the problem isn't the lack of opportunities for creative entrepreneurs like Carolyn Gallagher. The problem is the deluge of options. In an environment where one is constantly tempted by unfilled niches, unsolved problems, and unmet needs, staying focused can be the biggest challenge of all. That's why it's important to define your personal and professional objectives early on and say no to anything that might pull you off course. As Carolyn says, "You have to make decisions based on the life you want for yourself. Otherwise, you're rafting down a river without a paddle, letting the current carry you along. You could end up anywhere."

Balance Family and Business

"Having a home office and being close to my kids was always my dream," Carolyn recalls. She found this was much easier to do in Argentina than in the United States. "Trying to run a business and raise a family back home is nearly impossible because hired help is so expensive. The experience can be overwhelming."

Fortunately, Argentines put great value on childrearing and the support network that helps parents balance their personal and professional lives. "Here, they understand that spending quality time with your kids is more important than doing house chores and that busy parents need all the help they can get," says Carolyn. "With good maids and nannies it is possible to achieve harmony between family and business."

To help maintain that sense of harmony, Carolyn decided to open her home office when her second daughter was born. In typical Argentine fashion, despite being located in what had been a garage, the office is large, impeccably furnished, and professional. "Julia was born in the middle of high season in January. So I hired support staff and got up and running in a space where we could all work and play together. When we hit the down season in May, we could finally catch our breath and be a family!"

Sometimes being a family means including children in business activities outside the home, but that hasn't been a problem for Carolyn. "I've given tours and language classes with one or both of my children present. People remember that and stop me on the street to ask how my kids are doing. Having children has actually helped me integrate into the community as a person and as a businesswoman."

Indeed, it's not only possible to achieve a healthy balance between work and family in countries where women play a more traditional role; it may in fact be easier to do so. Thanks to affordable help and a child-centric culture, men and women can be both successful entrepreneurs and parents in Argentina. "The people I've hired understand that I need help to get things done with my family and my business. I'm really grateful for that," Carolyn says.

Find Inspiration

To stay focused and motivated as an expatriate entrepreneur in Argentina, Carolyn keeps two inspirational writings close at hand. One is an anonymous poem titled "Dream Big"; the other is a short essay by Hunter S. Thompson called "Security." Carolyn felt so strongly about these writings that she sent copies to me so I could better understand her story. "I want to share with you the inspirational pieces that have been such powerful influences in my life," she wrote in her e-mail.

"Dream Big" is often presented to students in the United States when they finish their high school or university studies, but it's just as relevant to entrepreneurs who are about to start a new life in a foreign country. "When I graduated from high school, my next-door neighbor gave me a beautiful poster of the 'Dream Big' poem," Carolyn recalls. "I liked it so much that I brought it with me to Argentina."

Carolyn found "Dream Big" to be particularly inspirational during the 2008 global financial crisis. At that time, tourists were purchasing low-cost services to fit their travel budgets rather than her company's custom-built tours. "It was the final price rather than personalized service that made the sale," she recalls. Carolyn was tempted to change her business model and simply be a concierge; but she spoke with a close friend, reflected on "Dream Big," and redoubled her efforts to find clients who valued the "little details" of her tours. Her determination paid off. Today, Uncorking Argentina is ranked number one among Mendoza tour operators on TripAdvisor. Carolyn says, "Thanks in part to 'Dream Big,' instead of packing up and leaving when I encountered problems, I kept going. It really has helped me to be successful."

When I interviewed Carolyn in her home office, "Security" was open on her computer screen. She reads it often to remind herself of why she decided to become an entrepreneur in an emerging market. "The essay really opened my eyes to the benefits of risk and the dangers of security," Carolyn says. "Security" reads in part:

> Turn back the pages of history and see the men who have shaped the destiny of the world. Security was never theirs, but they lived rather than existed. Where would the world be if all men had sought security and not taken risks or gambled with their lives on the chance that, if they won, life would be different and richer?

Whether the source is a poem, an essay, or the life story of an adventurous friend or relative that provides encouragement, you need inspiration to help you overcome the challenges of starting a business in an emerging market. As Carolyn observes, "Life is going to take turns, just as a river turns. There are rocks here and there, the water level rises and falls, and there are eddies and whirlpools. Inspiration, like a good raft, is something to cling to when things get rough."

Dream Big

If there were ever a time to dare,
To make a difference
To embark on something worth doing
It is now.
Not for any grand cause, necessarily—
But for something that tugs at your heart
Something that is worth your aspiration
Something that is your dream.
You owe it to yourself
To make your days count.
Have fun. Dig deep. Stretch.

Dream big.

Know, though,
That things worth doing
Seldom come easy,
There will be good days
There will be bad days
There will be times when you want to
Turn around
Pack it up
and call it quits
Those times tell you
That you are pushing yourself
And that you are not afraid to learn by trying.

Persist.

Because with an idea,
Determination and the right tools,
You can do great things.
Let your instincts, your intellect
And let your heart guide you.

Trust.

Believe in the incredible power
Of the human mind
Of doing something that makes a difference
Of working hard
Of laughing and hoping
Of lasting friends
Of all the things that will cross your path

The start of something new
Brings the hope of something great.
Anything is possible
There is only one you
And you will pass this way but once.

Do it right.

—Author unknown

Use Technology as a Force Multiplier

Carolyn keeps her business small to maintain the personal touch her clients value and to achieve harmony between family and work. She is able to do so in part by using technology as a force multiplier. "Ten years ago, I would have needed printed materials and a person in charge of marketing and sales. Thanks to digital technology, I can do everything myself. All I need is an Internet connection and a business card," Carolyn explains. To that end, she has a Vonage voice over IP (VoIP) phone with a toll-free number in the United States that rings at her home office in Argentina. "Potential clients can find me quickly and easily; they just pick up the phone and call me for free." Carolyn also relies on her Web page and sites like TripAdvisor to promote her services. "I wouldn't exist without the Internet," she admits.

Because of technology, it is less time-consuming and expensive to promote your business to a global market. And living in a place like Argentina doesn't mean being isolated from the developed world and its knowledge centers. Thanks to e-book readers like Kindle, Internet sites like WebMD, and satellite services such as DirecTV, news and information are more accessible than ever. "I feel included in the world," notes Carolyn. To illustrate, Carolyn offers this story: "When Carmen got sick last month my husband told me she had probably eaten unrefrigerated ice cream. So, I got on the Internet, looked up her symptoms, and found medical advice in English that put me at ease. The ability to quickly access reliable information allows me to be efficient, as well as to dedicate more time to my family."

As you are contemplating doing business in an emerging market, consider the role that technology can play in promoting your services, minimizing overhead, and keeping you informed. Correctly leveraged, technology can help you achieve your goals no matter the scale or physical location of your venture.

Conclusion
Less Can Be More

As a river guide, mother, and entrepreneur, Carolyn Gallagher has always managed to keep her balance. She does so by dreaming big but staying small—and carefully moving step-by-step toward her goals. "I believe in what I'm doing. Even though my business might not grow exponentially, I'm having fun," she says.

Carolyn's story shows us that being an expatriate entrepreneur in an emerging market is about much more than running a business. It's also about creating a new life for oneself. Carolyn didn't have to raise a million dollars, chase every business opportunity, or open a fancy office. She just had to put her heart in her business, her car in the street, and her office in the garage. By doing so, at least a couple of days a week she can say to her girls, "Let's go to the park! Let's go play games and finger paint!" For Carolyn, that's true success.

LESSON 4

Choose the river you will raft or the mountain you will climb based on your professional *and* personal goals. Then scout the territory to see what you should do to prepare for the journey. Remember, in an emerging market it may be easier to reach your objectives if you travel light.

5

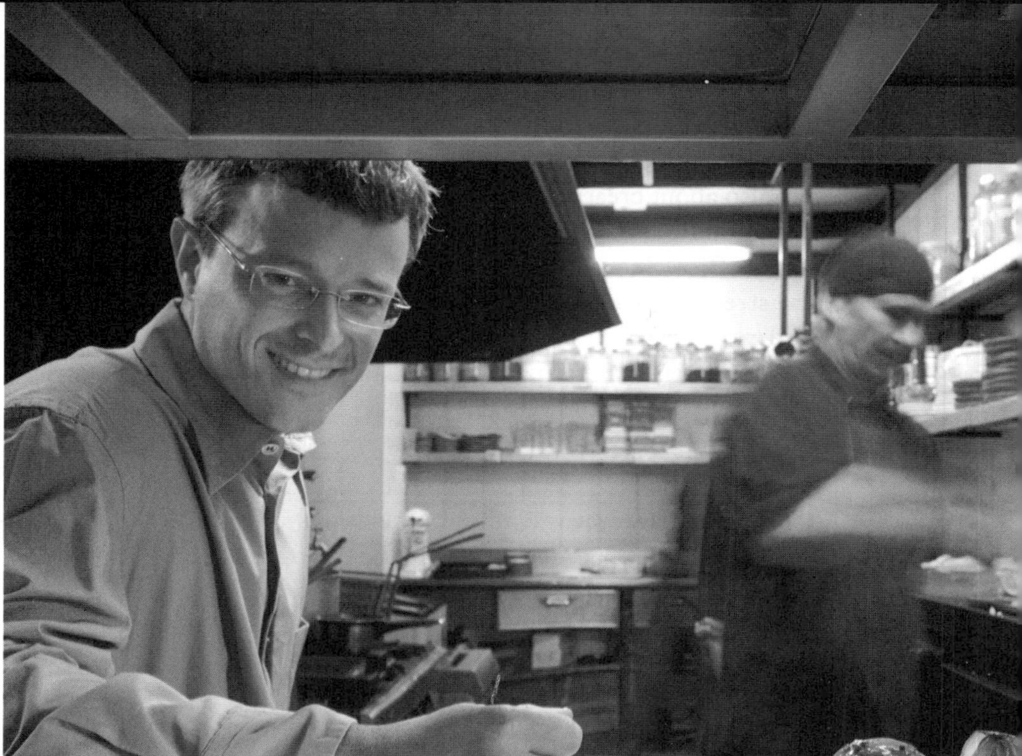

The Patient Fisherman

*"You can't be in a hurry. Opportunity comes when waiting
for the right time to do the right thing."*
—JEROME CONSTANT

"**W**hen is he *finally* going to open that restaurant?"
We had been asking ourselves this question ever
since Jerome Constant attended the first meeting of the Mendoza Expats Club in September 2005. Every month, he told us that Anna Bistró was "really coming along" and would open *"prochainement"* (soon). It seemed like it was taking forever, and we were desperate for a place to eat that served more than French fries and *milanesa* (fried, breaded veal, one of Argentina's most popular dishes).

What we did not know was that Jerome Constant is an avid fly fisherman, so much so that he proclaims, "I can't live in a country where the fishing isn't really good." Therefore, like a patient fisherman, Jerome was taking his time to ensure conditions were ideal before opening the doors to his new business. His patience paid off. Today, Anna Bistró is a favorite among not only foreign tourists and residents but locals as well, including the former governor of Mendoza and current vice president of Argentina, Julio Cobos.

Raised in Paris, Jerome comes from a family of independent professionals. His father is an architect, and his uncles are lawyers.

Jerome majored in finance, yet he received a broad education in, as he describes it, "everything that relates to running a company, from law and accounting to marketing and strategy."

At eighteen, he made the conscious choice to become an entrepreneur someday—but only when the right opportunity came along. "It had to be something that made sense and that I could do well," he says.

Although Jerome considered starting businesses in various industries in France, he couldn't find a concrete project. Still, he didn't give up hope of one day landing *the big one*. "When my friends started working, they took the 'logical' next steps of buying a home, taking on twenty years of debt, and so on. I never wanted that. I wouldn't have had the money to invest in my dream if an opportunity presented itself."

When he was given the chance to relocate to Canada in 2001, Jerome jumped at it. "I went to work for a French firm that sold dynamic outdoor billboards in North America. I spent a year and a half in Toronto and Montreal restructuring the company to solve its financial problems and improve profitability."

While he was in Canada, Jerome explored his two passions. "I went out to Alberta and British Columbia to fish. However, I also looked at land," he recalls. His idea was to develop a business connected to a real estate investment. The problem was, even building a small house cost between US$300,000 and $400,000. "After spending that much, I wouldn't have had anything left to invest."

While working in Toronto in 2003, Jerome saw on the Internet that Argentina had gone from being the most expensive country to visit in Latin America to one of the cheapest. And the stories he read in his beloved fly-fishing magazines constantly reminded him that "for a true fanatic, it's a dream to fish in Argentina." So Jerome decided to quit his job and test the waters in the land of Tango and Brown Trout. "I said to myself, 'Move now. Try. Do something. It will work or it won't, but at least *try*.'" In January 2004, traveling by bus from Chile, he arrived in Junín de los Andes, one of Argentina's fishing hot spots. From there he traveled south all the way to Ushuaia, but after four months he decided to go to Mendoza because a friend in the French wine business had told him it was the center of Argentina's wine industry and worth a visit.

When he arrived in Argentina in early 2004, Jerome wanted to invest. But, like many first-time entrepreneurs, he didn't know exactly where to put his money. "I searched for ideas adapted to the country, where I could use my abilities," he remembers.

At first, Jerome partnered with a French couple in El Bolson to export Patagonian mushrooms to Europe. However, because he was based in Mendoza and that business was located fourteen hours south by car, it didn't provide the lifestyle he was looking for. "I can't be successful in my professional life without considering my personal life as well," he says. So he kept searching.

While he was spending time in Mendoza, Jerome noticed that real estate was inexpensive. "I saw large properties for sale very close to the city center and thought, 'There is opportunity here.'" He also recognized an "incredible dynamic" around wine, skiing, mountain climbing, and great weather. "Mendoza was attractive as an international tourist destination and wine capital, and it had tremendous potential for growth. There was also land that cost next to nothing only seven hundred meters from Plaza Independencia [the center of the city]."

From his background in finance, Jerome knew that the value of real estate so close to a vibrant urban core almost never stays low for long. So he purchased an undeveloped lot about six blocks from the central business district, although he had no idea what he was going to do with it. "Initially, I saw it simply as a real estate investment in which I couldn't possibly lose," Jerome explains. "Nonetheless, I was careful not to put all my savings into the property. I set a part of them aside to do other things."

During a trip to Buenos Aires, Jerome came up with the idea for Anna Bistró. "I met French people there who had opened highly successful restaurants. I saw that size was key. If the establishment was large enough, you could organize, structure, and delegate. That's one reason I decided to start a restaurant instead of another type of business. I didn't want to be a slave to my investment." In short, Jerome likes to go fishing and then to have the time to eat the fish he catches.

On March 22, 2006, Anna Bistró opened, and Mendoza's expatriate community finally had a new place to dine. Jerome's restaurant was like no other in town. He had created a stunningly beautiful building from scratch with huge picture windows, a high parabolic roof, local artwork hanging on warmly colored brick walls, and capacity for more than one hundred diners. Seating on the inside was almost as airy and open as in the large garden outside. The menu offered salads, entrées, and desserts that were a refreshing change from pizza, empanadas (meat-filled pastries), and *milanesa*. There was even free Wi-Fi, and foreign tourists could order lunch or dinner at nearly any time of the day (otherwise unheard of in Mendoza). Jerome had cast his line wisely.

So, just how did a Frenchman with a penchant for finance and fishing end up running one of the most successful restaurants in Mendoza? Let's take a closer look at his story.

Be Different

Jerome lived in Mendoza for eight months before he decided to open a restaurant, patiently taking his time to get his bearings and find the right opportunity. His first venture had been exporting fresh *morilles* mushrooms to Europe. But he did not like the lifestyle the business offered him, and he also realized, "there weren't many ways to differentiate myself. It was a mature market with a lot of players."

While he was deciding what to do next, Jerome was eating in local restaurants and becoming painfully aware of their deficiencies. "There was nowhere I could have a decent salad at 6:00 P.M. while sitting outside amongst green plants. On the first day in town, you're thrilled to eat a big thick steak, but on the seventh day you say, 'It's 38 degrees [100 degrees Fahrenheit]. I want some fresh vegetables!' " Even though most of the ingredients for a Mediterranean-style salad are homegrown in Mendoza, in many local restaurants salads were not available as a main course. That realization became the basic idea behind Anna Bistró.

Jerome's friends and family back in France thought it was crazy for someone who had never been a restaurateur to start a restaurant in Mendoza, Argentina. "In a family of French doctors, the sons are doctors. In a family of lawyers, they are lawyers. Change of profession isn't easily accepted," he explains. "We don't have the openness or flexibility found in the Anglo-Saxon world." However, Jerome succeeded in part because he was "crazy" enough to go to a place where he and his ideas were unique. "The main reason I've been successful here is that I'm different from everyone else, and so is my business."

In addition to a lack of European-style salads and fare other than meat and pasta, there were few restaurants in Mendoza that fully integrated location, interior design, menu, and service. The goal of Anna Bistró was to bring all these elements together. About the concept, Jerome observes, "Packaging is as important as product. It generates a feeling within you. It communicates something. I saw this in Paris fifteen years ago with the renovation of the clothing stores, cafés, and bakeries. These days, branding extends to the physical establishment. It's no longer just the product."

An all-encompassing concept of branding was indeed foreign to most of Mendoza's restaurateurs. Ironically, a fisherman from France proved himself ideally suited to introduce it to the market. Why? "In a distant country, proven business concepts from back home are often new to the locals. Therefore, implementing them is less costly and less risky than developing an enterprise from scratch. Think about the bakeries French immigrants have opened around the world. It was a lot easier for them than starting a bakery back in France."

Like the French bakers, Jerome's story shows us that it can be easier for entrepreneurs to distinguish themselves outside their country than within it. "I never would have opened a restaurant in France because the competition is too stiff," he says. "In France, I would just be another Frenchman." In emerging markets like Argentina there are countless opportunities for people with novel ideas and an outsider's perspective. As Jerome says, "If you know how to leverage your uniqueness, there aren't many reasons to fail."

Listen for Gunfire

Jerome's investment philosophy is built on his grandfather's favorite saying: "Buy when you hear gunfire, and sell when you hear violins." It's an allusion to the economic cycles of nations, products, industries, and companies that Jerome took to heart at a young age. "The point is that wise investing is countercyclical and counterintuitive. If things have been going badly, it's time to invest even though your natural instincts tell you to do the opposite. This is especially true for operations in financially driven markets like real estate."

In other words, be wary of countries that have had five to ten years of steady growth. "That's the riskiest time to invest," according to Jerome. Indeed, he knew in his blood that he would find the best opportunities in an emerging market that had recently suffered an economic collapse. "If the 2001 crisis in Argentina hadn't happened, I wouldn't be here. That's for sure."

In addition to depressed real estate values, Jerome believes that a devalued currency is also a big help in building a new business and a new life overseas. "To start a worthwhile project in France, you need half a million euros or more. And, you must have significant resources to finance yourself for the year and a half that it takes to get up and running. When I arrived in Argentina, I spent only 450 euros [then about US$540] per month on living expenses. That gave me peace of mind to think and develop my ideas without pressure. Back home, you needed at least 2,500 euros [then about US$3,000] per month just to live, not to mention all the expenses involved in starting a business."

Following the 2001 financial crisis, Argentina was basically on the auction block. The For Sale signs on countless homes, apartments, store windows, and farms revealed the locals' pessimism and their fear that things would get even worse. Most of them were too busy shaking their heads to look up and see the extraordinary opportunities around them. They were selling with the sound of gunfire because they thought the violins would never play again. Jerome Constant knew better and invested against the trend.

As you contemplate your venture, be aware of economic cycles and judge whether your target emerging market is likely near an economic peak or a valley. Despite what the majority may say or do, launching a business at a time when an economy is so depressed that it can only go up is one way to ensure maximum return on investment. Investing during the good times may seem "safe," but it is often only a guarantee of mediocrity.

Hedge Your Bets

A hotel was the first business Jerome considered for the plot of land he purchased near Mendoza's city center. However, the cost to build it was so high that it would have required investment partners. For Jerome, it was "too much money and too much risk."

Initially, he discarded the idea of a restaurant because "it seemed like a profession of indentured servitude." Then he went to Buenos Aires and learned that the income from a French bistro of sufficient size could justify hiring a manager. He also ran the numbers and saw that the cost of building and furnishing Anna Bistró would be roughly equal to the value of his land. That was a turning point. "I knew that if I got into trouble, I could just sell the property and be debt free. That insight gave me the security to do the project," he says.

In other words, if you start a business and it doesn't work, that's one thing. It's quite another if the business doesn't work and you are also left with debts to pay back over the next twenty years. "With the restaurant, I couldn't lose," Jerome explains. "If it failed, I could still go back to work in Europe. It wouldn't have been such a grave mistake."

When Jerome tells his story, he focuses on the financial aspects, saying, "I always knew it would be a lot easier to do things with a smaller budget and less financial risk in an emerging market." As any financial expert would, he hedged his risky restaurant bet with an underlying asset of inherent value. Jerome explains that in France the concept is known as *investissement foncier.* "It means an investment tied to the land."

The benefits of *investissement foncier* can be seen in Argentina's grape-farming industry, where selling grapes to wineries is only marginally profitable over the long term (losing part or all of a year's harvest to hail, frost, disease, or ravenous insects puts a serious dent in one's ten-year numbers). However, if the farmers' timing is right, their land appreciation is so great that many years of business losses can be offset by the sale of their property when the violins are playing. Remember: Real estate appreciation can be a savior when profit doesn't materialize from a business venture. Nowhere is this truer than in emerging markets like Argentina, where shorter economic cycles have created more opportunities to buy low and sell high.

Be Realistic and Flexible

Having realistic expectations based on the local culture is key to success as an expatriate entrepreneur in an emerging market. Thinking things will function as they do back home is a mistake. Jerome explains, "On a personal level, the Argentines are always agreeable and casual. The challenge is that they're the same at work. It's common for an employee to say she'll arrive at 8:00 A.M. but then not show up or even call with an excuse. Vendors don't have fixed delivery hours. If they don't come, they don't call. Sometimes you wonder who's the vendor and who's the client!"

The informality that permeates Argentine culture means an expatriate entrepreneur often must work harder to get the same results as in North America or Europe. As Jerome has learned, "You need a lot of patience, creativity, and energy to adapt to the local work ethic. You can demand a little more formality, but you can't go too far or it becomes counterproductive. The locals simply won't understand or accept it."

To integrate successfully with employees and vendors, Jerome realized that he had to adapt to the Argentines rather than expecting the Argentines to adapt to him. Otherwise, it's like "trying to hold back the waves of the ocean," he says. How did he do it? "I organized myself in such a way that I'm not waiting for everybody else to show up. Everybody else is waiting for *me*." In other words, Jerome anticipates. "You have to take into account that when you ask for something to be delivered in January, it's sure to arrive in March or April. Nobody is going to apologize or admit that it should have been delivered in January. You must plan accordingly and base your expectations on the local culture."

The need to be realistic about cultural differences goes beyond Jerome's relationship with Argentines. He also recognizes the differences among the people who eat at his restaurant: "North Americans don't have the same expectations as Italian, French, English, or Dutch customers. For some nationalities, service is absolutely fundamental. For others, it's all about the quality of the food. The locals care about the heating tubes [which allow for outdoor dining in the winter], while many clients from overseas don't think it ever gets cold here and therefore don't care about them at all." It's a cultural juggling act that requires customer feedback to keep everyone happy. "Feedback is essential to understanding your weaknesses from each culture's viewpoint. I constantly read our reviews on TripAdvisor and often find myself saying, 'Well, they are right about this issue from the perspective of an Italian. Unfortunately, they are right, and something must be done!'"

Over the past decade, I've seen that unrealistic expectations are one of the main causes of frustration among foreigners doing business in Argentina. Many investors think that their way of doing things is the most efficient and just can't understand why the locals don't agree. What's important to keep in mind is that a reed will only bend so far before breaking. It might be possible to make superficial modifications to the behavior of employees or partners, but their underlying culture will not change. Recognize this fact and be flexible enough to modify *your* behavior accordingly.

Be a "Sarmiento"

"Patience and persistence are how I handle it." That's Jerome's response when he is asked about the infamous Argentine bureaucracy, where it's common to file the same application three times and be asked each time to provide completely different supporting documentation. "In the beginning, I did everything myself in order to save money. I stood in a lot of lines!" he says.

Jerome was so persistent that at town hall he earned the nickname "Sarmiento," a reference to the educational reformer and nineteenth-century Argentine president known for his tenacity. "I was there waiting when they opened the door each morning. Every time they told me I had to return with more documents, I got them and came running back immediately. They couldn't believe it."

The Argentines themselves talk about *el no fácil*, or "the easy no." That is how they describe the frustrating tendency some have to say no to any and all requests. As Jerome explains, "Bureaucrats are always looking for excuses to say, 'No, it's not possible,' or 'You can't do that.'" His solution? "You have to get to the bottom of their reasoning by asking 'why?' until they discover for themselves that their argument is illogical. In 90 percent of the cases they are capable of solving your problem. If you give up after their first response, you don't get anywhere. They tell you that you have to see another person, or that it won't work, or that you have to come back tomorrow. However, most of the time, it isn't so. They *can* solve your problem. You just have to be persistent."

Tenacity is one of the secrets to success in any endeavor anywhere in the world. However, the bureaucracy in many emerging markets puts expatriate entrepreneurs' patience to a tough test. Whereas a company can be formed online in a matter of hours or even minutes in many parts of the developed world, it can take months in Argentina. As you begin your journey, take a deep breath and reset your expectations. You will achieve your objectives only if you are patient and persistent.

Invest in Technology

Today, technology plays a fundamental role at Anna Bistró, but it didn't start out that way. "We began with the simple idea of differentiating ourselves by putting tables in the middle of a garden and offering an original menu," Jerome says. "We purchased almost all the kitchen equipment, chairs, tables, and furnishings at auction in Buenos Aires to keep our costs low in the beginning." His plan was to limit initial financial risk and, once up and running, to invest in technology. Now that Anna Bistró is a bona fide success (to accommodate increased demand, seating capacity has doubled since opening day), he's doing just that.

As of this writing, Jerome is completing a state-of-the-art wine cellar beneath the restaurant where not even a basement existed before. Another innovation consists of the gas heating tubes he has installed above the tables on the outside deck. According to Jerome, "We installed them so customers can eat outside year-round. Since it's now against the law to smoke inside, the system lets us create a space where smokers can eat and smoke in peace, even in the winter. That technology alone drives a lot of our business." More than 58 percent of Anna Bistró's total revenue comes from its outside tables. And thanks to seasonal changes in clientele (more tourists in the summer and more locals in the winter) as well as innovative seating options, revenue is stable throughout the year. "In addition to the heated deck for smokers, we have the wine cellar in winter, the gardens whenever the weather is nice, and the air-conditioned salon in the summer," explains Jerome.

Jerome also implemented a touch-screen ordering system for his waitstaff. Such technology is common in North America and Europe but is a competitive differentiator in the Mendoza market. It has made a huge difference in productivity, error reduction, and overall quality of service at the restaurant. "The system lets our waiters spend more time attending their customers. It reduces error, because the order printouts give us better oversight. And, it's a lot harder for a waiter to steal by billing a table without putting it in the system. It's a wonderful technology because it allows us to focus on improving service and quality."

On the subject of technology, Jerome highlights the importance of differentiation: "Technology is essential to being better than your competitors. It solves internal problems that don't make a difference to the customer but frees up time so you can focus on what does." Indeed, just like your unique background and skills, technology can be a wonderful tool for setting your emerging market business apart from the crowd.

Conclusion
The Patient Fisherman on a Lonely River Catches More Trout

Jerome's story is rich in lessons on success: Differentiate yourself from competitors, buy when most people are selling, build a business on top of an appreciating real estate asset, and find a place where start-up costs are low. While these lessons are applicable almost anywhere business is conducted, they are especially relevant and powerful in emerging markets.

After all, your idea to sell fish and chips is more likely to be something special in Brazil than back home in England where there are a million fish-and-chip shops. Boom-and-bust cycles have historically been shorter in emerging markets, so there are more opportunities in those countries to buy "at the sound of gunfire." The lower lows following crises in places like Argentina also mean that real estate can appreciate much more quickly than in the developed world. And, thanks to favorable exchange rates, your savings will likely go a lot further in Buenos Aires than in Boston.

Jerome's success certainly validates the strategy of casting a line in distant and relatively unexplored waters. But it teaches another, equally important lesson: Don't decide what bait to use until you have taken the time to get to know the place where you are fishing. Patience and a readiness to seize opportunity, to know when to reel in the line, are equally essential to success.

When I asked Jerome for analogies between business and fishing, he said, "There are many types of businessmen, just as there are many types of fishermen. I am a totally dedicated fisherman who focuses completely on the work of fishing. Fishing, like business, is a subtle game of observation and adaptation to the conditions at any given moment. That sense of observation helps me to make the right decisions at the right time, on the river and in my business."

LESSON 5

Business, like fishing, is all about location and timing. Doing business in the wrong market or moving at the wrong moment could mean you catch a tadpole instead of a trout.

A Stranger in His Own Land

GUSTAVO'S STORY

*"Having a unique perspective has been
essential to my success."*
—GUSTAVO ESPITIA

In Mexico they think of him as a gringo, but in Argentina he's considered a *mejicano*. When he returns to Mexico City, his friends say he acts like an Argentine. No matter where he goes, Gustavo Espitia is a stranger in his own land. That's part of his secret to success.

Today, Gustavo and his wife, Leticia, own and operate Aguamiel (which means "Honeywater"), one of Mendoza's most successful rural boutique hotels. It features stunning, environmentally friendly architecture, an organic vineyard, a superb restaurant, and owners who greet you at the door when you arrive. *Lugares*, an Argentine travel magazine, was so impressed it raved, "Aguamiel's quality is apparent in every detail of the hotel." Indeed, there is no other place in Mendoza quite like it. Nor is there another hotel owner quite like Gustavo Espitia.

Growing up, Gustavo barely knew other Mexican kids because he attended an American school in Mexico City. "My parents recognized that English was the global language of business and that if I learned the language of business, I would also learn the culture of business," he recalls. "So I studied in the United States—in Mexico."

Gustavo went on to study at Universidad Iberoamericana in Mexico City and then Harvard, where he earned a master's degree in architecture in 1998.

At the age of thirty, Gustavo joined the team in charge of extending Mexico City's subway system. It wasn't long before the Harvard-educated architect with American values experienced a culture clash with his fellow Mexicans. "I had trouble adapting to my own country because I had been educated in an Anglo-Saxon bubble," he says.

In fact, chairs were thrown and punches were pulled at a public meeting when Gustavo accused subway contractors of caring more about money than the welfare of Mexico City. "They wanted to beat me up right in front of the mayor!" he recalls. To resolve the dispute about where new lines should be built, the city decided to bring in two consultants from the Paris subway system. One of them was a beautiful young Argentine woman named Leticia. With a sheepish grin Gustavo admits, "In the end, even I had a personal agenda with the subway." He and Leticia were married two years later.

After nearly a decade of working on Mexico City's subway expansion, Gustavo was approaching burnout. The pressure of his job was so intense that he developed a hernia between his stomach and esophagus that was usually seen only in elderly men. "The doctors would say to me, 'Turn off your cell phone for one hour each day,' and I would say, 'I can't. I help run the subway.' Then, they would say, 'Close yourself in your office for just thirty minutes, and don't answer the phone,' and I would say, 'I can't. I help run the subway.' There was always a broken water line, an exploding gas main, or some other catastrophe that demanded my immediate attention."

When Gustavo finally made the firm decision to leave his position, his boss put Gustavo's letter of resignation in his desk drawer and said, "The only person who has the power to quit is me! Now, get back to work!" In the end, Gustavo virtually had to walk off the job. "I was the only person in the history of the subway to voluntarily leave my position," he recalls.

At first, Gustavo and Leticia considered moving to Paris, where Leticia had a consulting opportunity, but they felt the environment there would not be ideal for their two young children. "Paris is wonderful, but it's a city where people care more about dogs and cats than kids," Gustavo says. Also, he felt there were too many rules and regulations in Europe. "You don't have to get twenty thousand permits to open a business in Argentina. In the wine industry, you can plant what you want where you want. If you feel like pulling up eighty-year-old vines, you just tear them out. Try that in France!"

The couple spoke to their friends and family about relocating to Leticia's homeland. Gustavo remembers, "The Mexicans said to us, 'Argentina is a crazy place. Don't go!' and the Argentines said to us, 'Argentina is a crazy place. Don't come!' So, it was obvious that we had to move there." The couple negotiated infrastructure-related consulting engagements with the city of Buenos Aires and moved in 2004. Two years later, they purchased a plot of land in the Mendoza countryside and started building Aguamiel.

Today, in addition to operating a successful hotel, Gustavo and Leticia are investing in the wine business. In 2010, they produced their first vintage; they are now in the process of building a small winery next to their hotel. "The wine will help us promote the hotel, and the hotel will help us promote the wine," Gustavo reasons, "since we already have a physical place to sell it."

How did a Harvard-educated architect go from working on one of the largest public-works projects in the world to owning a tiny hotel in an emerging market and, in the process, find personal and professional fulfillment? Read on to find out.

Speak with a Funny Accent

In 2004, when Gustavo left Mexico and started working as a consultant to the city of Buenos Aires, he quickly concluded that the Argentine government had privatized to the point of excess. "The government didn't even issue passports and driver's licenses anymore," he says. This meant that Gustavo had to learn to negotiate in an environment where private city service providers had all the power.

One Monday at 9:00 A.M., Buenos Aires' privately run water department, Aguas Argentinas, began digging a hole in the middle of a major intersection. "They closed off everything with no advance warning. Of course, the city exploded," remembers Gustavo. The mayor also exploded when images of furious *porteños* hit the airwaves. He ordered the city's director of infrastructure and Gustavo to fix the problem immediately.

Gustavo asked his secretary to get the head of Aguas Argentinas on the phone and tell him, "The Buenos Aires city government is calling. Come *now*!" No one at Aguas Argentinas would even take Gustavo's call.

In Mexico, when Gustavo called people to his office, they arrived two hours in advance—even the country's most powerful business leaders. "I *was* the state, and because the state provided and paid for everything, the private sector respected me. In Argentina, privatized companies provide and charge for services. So the state gets zero respect," he says.

However, Gustavo did find that when he was dealing with certain interest groups, he could in fact get respect—simply because he had a strange accent. "The locals just couldn't understand how it was that a Mexican was part of the Argentine government. Out of curiosity, even protesters would stop banging their pots and pans and listen to me when I spoke! In Argentina, foreigners really stand out. You may be a nobody back home, but, here, it's like, 'Wow!' You're special. And for no reason other than that you speak with a funny accent." As a result, whenever there was a protest outside his office building in Buenos Aires, city officials yelled, "Send Gustavo!"

Dealing with daily crises in the Buenos Aires government wasn't exactly what Gustavo had aspired to when he left Mexico City. However, the story of his first years in Argentina illustrates that it can be an advantage to stand out from the crowd. Even something as simple as a different accent can hold people's attention, make them remember you, and help get results when others can't.

Be the Valued Outsider

Gustavo's experience working for Mexico City, a municipality twice the size of Buenos Aires, was invaluable to his success as a consultant to Argentina's biggest city. One important insight was realizing that few politicians in Argentina had experience with governing. "They weren't used to solving problems themselves," he says. In an airport-planning meeting, a government minister described a problem as so complex that surely the only one who could resolve it was an urban planner from Barcelona. The mayor of Buenos Aires asked Gustavo for his opinion. "I told him that if a minister had said that in Mexico City, it would have been his last day on the job. Barcelona is the size of a Buenos Aires *neighborhood*. How could someone from there understand the scale of a problem in Buenos Aires?"

In Argentina, where government employees are usually considered inefficient and other Latin Americans are viewed with suspicion, Gustavo should have been at a disadvantage. However, his background in dealing with disasters on a daily basis in Mexico City qualified him to help solve some of Buenos Aires' toughest problems. Indeed, in many developing countries outsiders are highly respected for their foreign education and work experience. Even if an expatriate entrepreneur doesn't have a degree from Harvard or a fancy job title, his studies and work history can be a tremendous asset.

Do Your Homework

Thanks to his "funny accent" and problem-solving skills, Gustavo was constantly in demand and overworked as an independent consultant to the city of Buenos Aires. Once again, he was close to burnout. He started to think about following his lifelong dream of running his own business, far from the chaos of big-city government. He wanted to do something in Argentina, but at first he wasn't sure exactly what that might be. "As an architect, I wanted to build something and then sell it. However, I didn't have enough money for a large project. It also seemed too risky at the time."

Gustavo's family was in the rum business in Mexico, so he knew the alcoholic-beverage industry and initially thought about making wine. He discovered, however, that most winery owners in Argentina had first made money in an unrelated business. "The wine industry here is high-risk, and you have to wait a long time for a payoff. You need a lot of capital to deal with the risk and instability. I didn't have that kind of money," he explains.

As part of his research process, Gustavo met with the Minister of Tourism in Buenos Aires. "He told me that Argentina's problem was a lack of infrastructure. In the interior of the country there were no flights between cities, no highways, and very few good hotels," Gustavo says. The conversation convinced Gustavo that the country had incredible potential for tourism. "Compared to Mexico, it's crazy how much there is yet to be done here. Argentina isn't saturated. This county is like the old 'Wild West.' It's a true frontier."

Gustavo also learned that most foreign visitors arrive in Argentina via Buenos Aires or Santiago, Chile. "I saw that Mendoza was an ideal stopping point between the two most important cities in the Southern Cone. Although it wasn't a huge metropolis, Mendoza wasn't a small town either. It was the perfect size and had the basic infrastructure to support tourism."

Based on his research, Gustavo decided to start a business that combined wine and hospitality. "I wanted to build a hotel because I was an architect. I wanted to be in the countryside. I wanted my children to have a better quality of life than the one I had in a big city. And, I wanted to be involved with wine making," he explains. So, Gustavo set out to build a few hotel rooms and then a small winery once the hotel proved successful. Aguamiel opened in December 2007.

Gustavo leveraged his skills as an architect and his experience as a project manager to create something unique in an underserved market. Before he began, he took the time to analyze different industries and speak to locals who were aware of the challenges and the opportunities. Then he thought about his personal needs and developed a project that offered him and his family a balanced lifestyle. Indeed, rather than rushing into a new project in an emerging market, it makes sense to first learn the lay of the land. Doing your homework will allow you to identify businesses with long-term potential that match your personal and professional needs as well as your skills.

Get Plenty of Advice

Gustavo received lots of advice about living and working in Argentina—whether he asked for it or not. "To this day, after having lived in this country for more than six years, people still talk to me as if I landed here yesterday," he says. Who was his main advisor when he first arrived in Argentina? "Everyone and no one!" he says. "Everybody, absolutely everybody, had advice for me."

Soon after he moved to Mendoza, Gustavo went to lunch at the home of a family friend. "An old man sitting at our table suddenly turned to me and said, 'I'm going to give you some advice in case you want to do well in this country. First, maintain the lowest profile you can. Second, when in doubt, don't pay.'" At the time, Gustavo had no idea what the man was talking about. Now that he has been through the trials and tribulations of building a hotel in Argentina, he realizes it was good advice. "Sometimes, when I'm walking along the street, I remember that old man and laugh. I didn't ask for his guidance, but I certainly understand it now. Especially if you are a foreigner, if you pay for something here without checking the details first, you run the risk of being overcharged."

Gustavo also received memorable yet unsolicited advice at a reception with an Argentine ambassador. As he recalls, "The ambassador asked me how I was doing with the Buenos Aires government. When he heard my frustrations, he felt compelled to give me some suggestions. He said, 'First, you must understand that Argentina isn't a country; it's an adventure. Second, you must understand that the only constant in this country is a lack of consistency. The only certainty is change.' Again, I didn't ask for the advice, but now I'm glad I got it. I've learned through experience that the ambassador was right: In order to cope, it's best to think of this country as one big adventure and expect things to change constantly."

At a meeting with the president of a leading Argentine bank, Gustavo unexpectedly learned something about Argentine culture. "I thought we were going to talk about his bank's services, but instead he told me he wanted to give me some advice. I thought, 'Oh, no. Here we go again . . . ' He started by telling me that when ATMs appeared in Argentina, locals viewed them with great skepticism because you inserted a card, entered a code, and money popped out. They thought that because it worked once, it couldn't possibly work twice! I learned that when things are going smoothly, Argentines tend to think, 'This will blow up any minute.' That really helped me understand the culture here and better deal with employees, contractors, and service providers."

Although he didn't seek advice at first, Gustavo eventually came to appreciate what the locals told him about life and work in Argentina. His experience highlights the importance of getting advice when one embarks on a new venture, especially in an unfamiliar land. We don't have to agree with or apply everything we hear, but it certainly doesn't hurt to listen to what the well-intentioned natives have to tell us. The seed of a new business or the solution to a seemingly insurmountable problem may lie in one of their insights or suggestions. At the very least, their words may be helpful in coping with new surroundings and the challenges that an expatriate entrepreneur faces in an emerging market.

Seek Solutions in Technology

"I couldn't have been successful in this industry ten years ago. Not many eight-room hotels were around then, because the tools didn't exist to make them profitable." That's how Gustavo responded when I asked him about the impact of technology on his business. Technology plays a critical role at Aguamiel in keeping personnel costs down, selling vacant rooms, and promoting the hotel overseas. "I do everything online in real time, including hotel management," explains Gustavo.

In the hotel industry, one measure of success is occupancy rates. To obtain a high occupancy rate at Aguamiel, Gustavo utilizes an innovative online service developed by a company in Cordoba, Argentina. "The airlines sell seats by flight, and I sell beds by room night. It's the same principle. The closer it gets to the night you want to stay at my hotel, the less expensive your bed will be if you booked it on the Internet." If Gustavo isn't fully booked several days in advance, he holds an online global auction of any unsold beds. "After all, if I don't sell a bed for a certain night, I'll never recover the loss," he says. In short, the Internet gives Gustavo a way to turn otherwise empty beds into profit centers. Ten years ago he wouldn't have had that capability.

Especially with small hotels that don't sell all their beds every night, it's also difficult to make a profit when one is faced with high fixed costs, such as labor. "Employees are my biggest challenge," Gustavo says. At Aguamiel, technology plays a role in addressing this problem as well. "In a country like Argentina, where labor costs are high and relations are conflictive, I have to do as much as I can with as few people as possible. Computers don't get pregnant, don't get sick, don't sue me, and don't give me excuses when there are problems." By automating certain aspects of his business, like reservations and check-out, Gustavo needs fewer employees.

When it comes to promoting Aguamiel, Gustavo relies almost exclusively on the Web. "I establish relationships with my clients via the Internet. Before they call me, they check me out online." Gustavo says he is often asked by locals how he gets tourists to choose to stay at his hotel in the middle of the Mendoza countryside. His response? "It's the Internet. Why the Internet? Because it has a global reach." It doesn't matter that Aguamiel is fifteen kilometers (9.3 miles) from the city, has no sign at its entrance, and doesn't advertise locally. As long as it has a website and is on Expedia, Best Boutique Hotels, and TripAdvisor, the hotel has a worldwide presence.

Of course, it's nothing new to say that technology is key to the success of a company or that it gives a small business global reach. What's not commonly known is that technology that is considered old hat or even obsolete in the developed world can be a competitive differentiator in the developing world for those who can afford it. (Because of high import tariffs, inefficient distribution systems, and lower purchasing power, a computer can cost three or four times more in an emerging market than in the United States or Europe.) "In Argentina, there's not a vision that technology should be accessible to everyone. It's seen as a luxury. So you can perform miracles, even with something that is outdated by first-world standards," Gustavo observes.

Aguamiel also sets itself apart through the use of environmentally friendly technology. In fact, Gustavo applied German building codes when he built the hotel, since local regulations didn't take sustainability into account. "It's amazing how many Europeans research the sustainable practices of the places they are thinking about staying. Some of our guests actually ask to see the certification stamps on the recycled materials we used to build the hotel," he says. Indeed, being environmentally friendly gives Aguamiel a tremendous advantage in the Mendoza market. As Gustavo explains, "We receive a lot of guests who considered larger and more luxurious hotels in town yet booked with us because we are green and our competitors are not. The concept of sustainability hardly exists in the local hospitality industry."

Taking advantage of state-of-the-art technology can help a new business reach potential customers anywhere on the planet, increase operational efficiency, and stand out from the competition. The technology that others take for granted back home can in fact make the difference between the success and failure of a business in an emerging market.

Conclusion
Embrace the Opportunity to Be Unique

Whether he was studying at an American school in Mexico, working with contractors on Mexico City's subway system, negotiating with protesters in Buenos Aires, or running a hotel in the Mendoza countryside, Gustavo has consistently been the odd man out. However, instead of being defeated by the difficulties that faced him as a minority of one, he stepped up to the plate and hit home run after home run.

Gustavo's story teaches us not to fear being a stranger in a strange land. Time and time again success came to him exactly *because* he was so different from everyone else. "Having a unique perspective has been essential to my success," he says. "Here in Mendoza, I've taken on the mother of all challenges. I've been able to do so because I have the Anglo-Saxon mentality of preparation, hard work, sacrifice, and personal integrity."

When I asked Gustavo where he would start a business if not in Argentina, he said, "Nowhere. I am in the place where I want to be, and this is my moment. If I had stayed in Mexico I would be an architect, and I would be insane." Ironically, back "home," Gustavo would be an outsider to the life he always dreamed about.

LESSON 6

Expatriate entrepreneurs perceive needs not visible to locals and address them using skills learned in other cultures and industries. Leverage your unique perspective as well as your education to compete in an emerging market like Argentina—and listen carefully when locals take the trouble to offer you advice.

7

Entrepreneur at Heart

ANNE-CAROLINE'S STORY

*"Being an entrepreneur has more to do with
who you are than where you are."*
— ANNE-CAROLINE BIANCHERI

Anne-Caroline Biancheri is a busy woman. Not only does she run one of Mendoza's most prestigious publishing companies, but she also owns a vineyard, an award-winning winery, and a boutique hotel. In addition to her professional life, she manages a household that includes two teenage boys. Although born in Marseille, Anne-Caroline has spent much of her life outside her native France. Because her father owned a transportation company, she and her family often found themselves calling places like the Ivory Coast home. "Traveling to so many countries at a young age was great preparation to be an entrepreneur in the developing world," she says.

Following her graduation from high school in Paris, Anne-Caroline studied publicity and marketing at a technical college. Two years later she embarked on her first entrepreneurial venture, a marketing firm she called ABC Communications. When the Gulf War put the French economy into a tailspin, Anne-Caroline was forced to close her business after only eight months. Her next move was to enroll in the American University of Paris, where she studied business and management.

To complete her business degree, Anne-Caroline had to obtain three elective credit hours. "I had been in Paris for seven years and was desperate to travel again, so I decided to do an internship overseas," she says. "Argentina seemed like the logical place to go, since my father owned a farm in Salta and had connections there." After three months as an intern at Manzi Publicidad in Buenos Aires, Anne-Caroline was offered a position at one of owner Carlos Manzi's companies that published magazines for Sheraton hotels and Aerolineas Argentinas. "I had finished my studies and was single, so I said to myself, 'Why not?'" she recalls.

At Manzi Publicidad, Anne-Caroline had her first experience producing a coffee-table book about a major tourist destination. It was called *Buenos Aires Night and Day*. While Anne-Caroline discovered she loved publishing, she didn't enjoy working for someone else. In September 1993, at the age of twenty-three, she launched her own firm, Caviar Bleu. "Argentina was the land of opportunity for me, not only because the people accepted me despite my young age but also because there was so much that hadn't yet been done. I don't think I would have gone back to France under any condition."

Besides being motivated by the sense of freedom and wide-open opportunities she found in an emerging market, Anne-Caroline admits that personal factors also played a role in her decision to stay in Argentina. "I was too proud to return home and tell my parents that I hadn't done well. I had something inside of me whispering, 'You said you were going to come here and do something, so do it!' I wanted to give it my best effort to see if I could truly make it on my own."

Although she set up her company in Buenos Aires, Anne-Caroline's first big project was in Santiago, Chile. In 1994, there were no coffee-table books about the city. So she produced one called *Santiago Cinco Estrellas* ("Five-Star Santiago"), which was marketed by Santiago's five-star hotels. "It was a great experience because I got to apply the skills I learned in Argentina in a completely different business environment," she says.

In 1998, Anne-Caroline moved from Buenos Aires to Mendoza to start a family, and she took Caviar Bleu along with her. In doing so, she discovered yet another untapped market. "Mendoza was a special place with a wonderful story and tremendous potential, yet no one had created a high-quality book to promote the area and to sell to foreign tourists. It was a great opportunity, just like Buenos Aires and Santiago had been."

Not only did she produce *Mendoza de Pura Cepa* ("Mendoza Through and Through"), the first coffee-table book about Mendoza and its people, but she also became involved in the wine business. In 1998, Anne-Caroline and her then husband purchased 126 hectares (311 acres) of land in the town of Vista Flores in Valle de Uco, about ninety-five kilometers (sixty miles) south of Mendoza. "It all began when we decided to buy a farm in the countryside where we could escape on the weekends with our young children," she remembers.

Anne-Caroline had no plans to make wine, but at the encouragement of a family friend, the famous French oenologist Michel Rolland, she planted 20 hectares (50 acres) of vineyard on her farm and built a small 140,000-liter winery in a simple shed. In 2003, she bottled her first vintage under the Antucura brand. In 2008, Anne-Caroline opened Casa Antucura, an eight-room boutique hotel in what had formerly been the family's residence during their weekend visits to the property. "Although I got into wine little by little and almost by accident, it turned out to be an interesting business," she says. "My ex-husband and I purchased the farm as a family project at a time when land in Vista Flores was less expensive and almost no one realized the area was ideal for growing high-end grapes. We were in the right place at the right time and fortunate to have the advice of a visionary like Michel Rolland."

In addition to good timing, an abundance of creativity, and an innate entrepreneurial spirit, what are Anne-Caroline's secrets to successfully running a publishing company as well as a vineyard, winery, and boutique hotel in an emerging market? The details of her personal story offer some helpful clues.

Travel to Build Character

Anne-Caroline says there are several reasons living overseas at a young age helped her to be successful as an expatriate entrepreneur in an emerging market. First, the experience gave her confidence. "When a family of four moves to a place like Africa, you learn to depend on yourself and on one another. That gives you the courage to take risks in life because you know you can be independent, but you also know you can count on your family's support."

Early exposure to other cultures also taught Anne-Caroline the importance of adaptability. "As a foreigner in a country that is completely different from your own, you aren't the one who makes the rules. You have to be open-minded and flexible in order to survive. There's no other way to do it."

Finally, she learned the advantages of having a unique perspective. At the launch party for *Santiago Cinco Estrellas*, the mayor of Santiago expressed surprise that a woman from France published the first book about his city. She told him it made perfect sense. She explains, "As a tourist I had searched for a coffee-table book on Santiago and couldn't find one. Most locals never would have realized there was a need."

Confidence, adaptability, and an outsider's perspective are essential for professional survival not only in a foreign country but also in a time of rapid change on a global level. "New markets appear suddenly and then quickly disappear. You have to have the capacity to see opportunities and reinvent yourself and your business accordingly. Those are skills you learn by traveling and by living in the developing world," notes Anne-Caroline.

You don't have to move to Africa when you're seven years old in order to later become an expatriate entrepreneur in an emerging market. However, success will come more easily if you have experience identifying unfulfilled needs and dealing with challenges such as culture shock. Whether it is an exchange program, internship opportunity, charity mission, temporary job posting, or family vacation, the sooner you expose yourself to the realities of the developing world the sooner you will be prepared to live and work there.

Don't Be Fooled by Appearances

Because of local charm, architectural beauty, or familiar customs, it's easy to be seduced into thinking that emerging markets like Argentina are actually in the developed world. However, as Anne-Caroline's experience shows, appearances can be deceiving. "Don't allow yourself to be fooled by sidewalk cafés and fancy Italian suits," she warns.

Despite her first impression that Argentina was European, Anne-Caroline found she had to work three times as hard as she would have in France to get Caviar Bleu on its feet. "There were lots of opportunities, but it took tremendous effort to take advantage of them. I learned that even though the locals look and in some ways act European, this is not Europe. Doing business in Argentina is an adventure."

In the beginning, incorporating a company, opening a bank account, and installing a telephone required a lot more of Anne-Caroline's time and energy than she had anticipated. "Creating a company in Europe takes three days. In Argentina it takes three months." Her experience with the phone company wasn't much better. She recalls that "it took *four* months to get a new line when I first moved here."

Thankfully, the privatization of state-run utilities has greatly improved the quality of telephone service, but the Argentine banking sector is still far from efficient. "Opening a checking account requires the endurance of a marathon runner," Anne-Caroline says. "And, when it's finally approved, the bank charges you a monthly fee for the privilege of lending it your money!"

Even though she says it feels much less European, Anne-Caroline had a more European experience doing business in Chile than in Argentina. "The Chileans may not dress like Europeans or tell you they are Italians who speak Spanish and act like the French, but in Santiago you can set up a business in two days and write checks without any problems. In Argentina, much of what passes for European is superficial."

A Portuguese in Brazil, an Italian in Argentina, and an Englishman in Kenya are all courting failure if they assume cultural similarities are an indication that business is done just as it is back home. In emerging markets you must be sure to look past superficial details. Speak to local experts about how things are done and why. You may discover that it takes four months to get a phone, but at least you will know enough to put your name on the waiting list.

Take the Plunge

Even though Anne-Caroline found that doing business in Chile was a more "European experience," her first foray into publishing would have been a dismal failure if it weren't for a skill she learned in Argentina. She calls it the "taking-the-plunge" approach to unexpected change.

"I was going to publish *Santiago Cinco Estrellas* in association with LADECO airlines, so I wouldn't have to open a subsidiary of Caviar Bleu in Chile," she explains. "Unfortunately, LADECO was sold just as the project was getting off the ground." When the airline called Anne-Caroline to say it couldn't honor its agreement with her, she found herself in a difficult and completely unforeseen situation. "At first, I wanted to curl up and die. I said to myself, 'This just can't be!'" She had already signed contracts with Sheraton, Hyatt, and the famous (now closed) Carrera hotel in Santiago. If she didn't follow through with the book, her image and her new company could be ruined. "What had been a small challenge suddenly became a huge one," she recalls.

Anne-Caroline's solution to the surprise turn of events was to do what any sensible Argentine would have done: react quickly and tackle the problem head-on. She rented a tiny office in a business center and asked her former colleagues at LADECO to recommend reliable lawyers and accountants to get Caviar Bleu Chile up and running. The company was formed in just fifteen days. "Chile's pro-business environment was a big factor to overcoming the challenge I faced, but so was my Argentine way of reacting to change," she recalls.

Argentines are indeed masters at responding to surprises. Their country's long history of economic booms and busts, as well as radical swings of the political pendulum, have taught them to be highly adaptable. It's an environment where the only certainty is uncertainty. "When the peso was devalued against the dollar in 2002, imported goods were suddenly three or four times as expensive as they had been. So the locals immediately started to make shoes, clothes, and all kinds of other products to sell domestically," Anne-Caroline explains. "If a similar crisis had occurred in France, it would have taken the people two years to figure out what to do!"

Especially in emerging markets, where economic and political turmoil have historically been a fact of life, reacting quickly to unexpected change is a crucial skill. If you find yourself in the deep end of the pool, it's sink or swim. Don't hesitate to change your strokes in order to stay afloat.

Serve Niche Markets

By publishing coffee-table books about Buenos Aires, Santiago, and Mendoza when no one had done so before, Anne-Caroline discovered markets in unexpected places. "It turned out that city and provincial governments were some of my best customers because they used my books as presents for visiting dignitaries," she says. This insight was key to the future success of Caviar Bleu. "In the beginning, I developed opportunities as they arose. Now, I carefully look for niches to fill."

Her company's current publications are indeed a reflection of Anne-Caroline's niche market philosophy. They include a handbook of Chilean wineries exclusively for guests of the Ritz-Carlton hotel in Santiago; a guide to hiking trails in Mendoza; and a collection of writings on Mendoza's history, culture, and economy. "Whenever I see that tourists or locals can't find information on subjects that interest them, I partner with experts and we produce a book to serve their needs," Anne-Caroline explains.

One area in which Anne-Caroline has identified a need is in the education of children with learning disabilities. "Project Pandora is a three-year initiative to develop five different products for a totally

virgin market that represents a significant portion of the population," Anne-Caroline explains. "I hired a group of specialists to study
and develop the concept. In doing so, I discovered that textbooks for
children with disabilities can actually be marketed to all kids, since
the specialized content promotes learning in untraditional ways."

In the area of tourism, Anne-Caroline is working on large-format
books about Argentine cities other than Mendoza. "A coffee-table
book on Salta doesn't exist. A coffee-table book on Rosario doesn't
exist. There's a tremendous opportunity there." She's also going
after other niches in tourism publishing with pocket-sized versions
of her best-selling titles. "Not everyone wants to buy *Mendoza de
Pura Cepa*," she says. "There's another segment of tourists that pre-
fers a smaller book at a lower price point."

Even in her wine business, Anne-Caroline takes a niche-market
approach. "The fact that we started off making blends across our
entire range of wines really helped us. No one else at the time was
doing blends at the lower end, so ours took off just like the coffee-
table books. Over the medium and long term, that's our strength:
occupying a space that is practically empty."

Whether with coffee-table books, children's textbooks, or
blended wines, Anne-Caroline is a specialist at marketing to niches
in order to maximize sales of her products. "If you fulfill an unmet
need and you do it well, success is a sure thing," she insists. As you
contemplate your emerging market business, be sure to research the
needs of your potential customers through focus groups, surveys, or
one-on-one interviews. Just like Anne-Caroline's success, *your* success depends in part on your ability to identify not only the size of
your market but also the many niches within it.

Mix Creativity with Flexibility

"Although perseverance is one way of dealing with the challenges
of running a business in an emerging market, sometimes you have
to use additional skills to solve problems," says Anne-Caroline.
According to her, one such skill is "creativity mixed with flexibility."

At Antucura, Anne-Caroline makes only the amount of wine she feels confident she can sell in a year. Therefore, the winery has idle production and storage capacity. Of course, she could just wait until sales improve to fill up her empty tanks. However, by being creative and flexible, Anne-Caroline has found a more profitable solution to the problem of unused assets. "I realized I was only going to need part of my infrastructure to produce a certain amount of my wine and that it would be ridiculous to not utilize the rest of it. So, I sat down and thought about an alternative," she explains.

The result of Anne-Caroline's flexible thinking was a creative agreement with Michel Rolland's Mendoza-based company, Eno Rolland. Rolland and his team now oversee Antucura's production in return for the right to make and store their own wines at the winery. Since the yearly cost of consultants like Rolland can run into the six figures, Anne-Caroline says, "It worked out perfectly to trade our extra capacity for the services of an industry expert."

Anne-Caroline also applied creativity mixed with flexibility to ensure the success of her boutique hotel. "I started Casa Antucura without having much experience in the hospitality industry," she admits. As a result, at the beginning, she struggled to make her family's former weekend residence a profitable eight-room hotel. "After the first year of operation I decided to temporarily close and think about options. That's when the idea of leasing the hotel to a third party came about," she says. An agreement was signed with a new management company in July 2010.

Anne-Caroline describes the process of thinking creatively about how to improve a business as mental gymnastics. "In the past, you only had to do the exercise every two or three years to keep a company going. Today, you almost have to do it monthly because of the speed of change in the market."

When you start your own business, remember to perform mental gymnastics by continually reviewing what you can do to make your operation more efficient. Your success depends on perseverance as well as creativity and flexibility. As Anne-Caroline advises, "Never consider something finished, even when it appears to be."

Take Advantage of Technological Advances

"Compared to when I started in 1993, technology has greatly changed the way in which I work. It's a vital tool for my businesses," Anne-Caroline notes. She credits e-mail with having the most impact overall. "It's reliable, quick, and inexpensive," she says. It's also the most efficient way for her to communicate with customers on a global basis. "I no longer send printed cards and invitations by mail. All of my communication is electronic."

Although Caviar Bleu still prints and sells books the old-fashioned way, the company is on the cusp of the latest technological trends in publishing. "We are using new formats such as the e-book to go after different niches and to complement traditional paperbacks," says Anne-Caroline. "It's not that regular books aren't being read anymore, but e-books are an excellent option for niche markets, since they can be published inexpensively and on demand just about anywhere."

Anne-Caroline is also developing dynamic websites for her books as a means of strengthening and maintaining relationships with customers—no matter where they are on the planet. "For our new title, *ABC Aconcagua* (named for the nearly 7,000-meter/23,000-foot mountain in the Andes between Mendoza and Chile), we're building a site where readers can interact with writers in order to ask questions, voice opinions, and tell their own stories about mountain climbing. In effect, anyone who enters the page becomes a participant in the book."

Technology has also played a big role in the distribution of Anne-Caroline's products. Even though her titles are sold throughout Argentina in more than eight hundred bookstores, they are also on Amazon. "It wouldn't make sense to put up my own website to sell books. I'd have to pay for links on search engines like Google just so customers could find us. Amazon is ideal because it gives our titles exposure to millions of customers around the world."

When Anne-Caroline launched Caviar Bleu more than fifteen years ago, she could only dream of the technology that would revolutionize the publishing industry. Today, it allows her to communicate inexpensively, create interactive online portals for her books, and distribute to an international customer base. To build an emerging market business with a global reach, be sure to incorporate the latest technological advances that are relevant to your industry. You will likely find, as Anne-Caroline did, that they are vital tools for your new venture.

Conclusion
Expose Yourself to the World

By living overseas at a young age and doing business in Argentina and Chile, Anne-Caroline learned to adapt, to "take the plunge," and to identify niches locals couldn't see. Thanks to those skills and her perspective as an outsider, she built several highly successful niche-market businesses in Mendoza.

Anne-Caroline's story demonstrates that success as an expatriate entrepreneur in an emerging market doesn't depend on external circumstances as much as on the personal attitudes and abilities you have developed over time. As she says, "There will be differences in what you can achieve in a given environment, but if you're entrepreneurial by nature you will be an entrepreneur wherever you are."

International experience does not mean a person has an international attitude, just as business experience does not necessarily mean a person has what it takes to be an entrepreneur. However, you can develop a global mind-set and an entrepreneurial spirit by traveling, making a genuine effort to understand and appreciate other cultures, and staying alert to unfulfilled needs that could present business opportunities. That's what Anne-Caroline did, and it made all the difference to her success.

LESSON 7

Moving to a foreign country and renting an office will not make you an entrepreneur in an emerging market. Only when you are able to see a nation and its people as they really are, and recognize niche opportunities, will you be ready for the journey. To prepare, travel or live overseas as early and as often as possible.

8

The Fortunate Fournier

JOSÉ MANUEL'S STORY

"If you come here with ideas set in stone, this isn't the place for you. You have to start from zero and build your business 'a la Argentina' if you want to succeed."
—JOSÉ MANUEL ORTEGA FOURNIER

You might say that José Manuel Ortega Fournier's success was "in the cards." His mother's family immigrated to Spain in 1785, where his ancestors used the lithography skills they had mastered in France to build a playing-card empire in their new homeland. Today, 95 percent of Spanish households and two thousand casinos around the world play with Fournier decks. José Manuel's paternal grandfather was also an entrepreneur in a foreign country. He moved from Spain to Salvador de Bahia, Brazil, during the Spanish Civil War. "We both came to South America in search of opportunity, although I did so under far better circumstances," says José Manuel.

Considering the entrepreneurial spirit in his genes, it's no surprise that José Manuel owns not one but three wineries, two of them in emerging markets. In 2002, he built his first near the town of San Carlos in Valle de Uco, just over one hundred kilometers (sixty miles) south of Mendoza. In 2004, he built a second in Ribera del Duero, Spain. And, in 2008, he completed the project with a winery in Maule, Chile. He explains, "My vision was to develop a wine-making business that united the Old World with the New at the top end of the market." As a fitting tribute to his heritage, the brand under which José Manuel sells his wine is O. Fournier.

The ace up José Manuel's sleeve is his wife, Nadia (who is also from Spain). She is an accomplished chef who runs both the restaurant at the Valle de Uco winery and the aptly named "Nadia O. F." restaurant in the Mendoza neighborhood of Chacras de Coria. It was in the Chacras restaurant that I sat down with José Manuel to talk about his experiences doing business in Argentina. While we spoke, Nadia spoiled us with her exquisite Spanish cuisine and several bottles of O. Fournier's legendary A Crux and B Crux wine. "From the beginning we had the idea to incorporate wine tourism into our project," José Manuel says. "This year we expect to do over AR$1.2 million [US$300,000] in business at the restaurant alone." That's an important milestone for José Manuel and Nadia, similar to when a business in the United States crosses the $1 million mark.

José Manuel's story begins with his birth in Burgos, Spain, in 1968, the same province his ancestors immigrated to from France, as well as the site of the second O. Fournier winery. "One of the objectives for my project," he explains, "was to purchase high-quality vineyards in Spain, and the place the Ortegas and the Fourniers come from just happens to have the best *terroir* [soil and climatic conditions] in the country."

In 1987, José Manuel lived overseas for the first time when he spent his senior year of high school in Mobile, Alabama, as an exchange student. Because he lived with an African American family, he returned to Spain with more than just a Southern accent. "I learned the importance of having an open mind and treating all people equally," he recalls. José Manuel would often draw on the lessons from his time in Alabama when he himself faced discrimination as a Spaniard doing business in Argentina.

After high school, José Manuel studied economics and political science at the Wharton School of the University of Pennsylvania.

"I learned to value relationships as well as the hard work that can help you achieve nearly any goal," he remembers. Because he was not wealthy, José Manuel also learned how to make the most of limited financial resources. "My key to survival as a poor college student was the discovery that you could freeze Big Macs!"

Following his graduation from Wharton, José Manuel was hired by Goldman Sachs to work in investment banking in London. As with high school and college, the experience would later prove valuable to him as an expatriate entrepreneur in an emerging market. "The spirit of client service Goldman practiced in the 1990s is ingrained in me," says José Manuel. "It's why at O. Fournier we have the philosophy that clients are always right and that their needs must be addressed immediately." To that end, José Manuel responds within an hour to 80 percent of the e-mails he receives. Even wine industry gurus like Jancis Robinson have commented on his work ethic. "Everyone I meet who has come across the dynamo behind O. Fournier agrees that José Manuel may just be the most hard-working wine producer in the world," she writes.

In addition to excellent client service, José Manuel demands perfection from himself and his employees. "At Goldman I learned to strive for excellence. So I encourage my staff to reach 100 percent of its goals. After all, if you aim for a ten you might hit a nine, but if you only aim for a nine, you might only hit an eight or even a seven," he notes. "Fighting mediocrity is like a long boxing match: you can never let your guard down."

From Goldman, José Manuel went to work at Santander Bank in London and Madrid, where he focused on the Latin American market. A friend in Buenos Aires who knew he was thinking about a venture in the wine business suggested he consider Mendoza. "I didn't know much about the area, so I visited in December 1999. There was tremendous potential because it was possible to produce high-quality wine in a low-cost environment," he says. In 2000, José Manuel purchased 260 hectares (643 acres) of land and planted 100 hectares (247 acres) of vineyard. Two years later, he opened a 1.2 million-liter winery on the site.

Although José Manuel jumped into a new industry in not one but three countries, without knowing exactly what the challenges would be, O. Fournier has been a success. Today, it is one of Mendoza's best-known tourist attractions and produces some of the region's highest-rated wines. Let's examine José Manuel's story to see how he overcame the challenges of doing business in Argentina and built a multinational wine brand that would make his entrepreneurial ancestors proud.

Choose Your Industry Carefully

There were many reasons why José Manuel decided to enter the wine business. In addition to the boom in Spanish wines during the 1990s, he liked the fact that wine making is usually done in the countryside. "I have always enjoyed the country more than the city," he explains. Also, José Manuel observed that wine had existed alongside mankind for thousands of years without significant change. "If you want to be an entrepreneur, and you're not a genius or a visionary, it makes sense to choose an industry that has a good chance of lasting longer than the fax machine or the telegraph," he notes.

Furthermore, José Manuel clearly saw the opportunity to form relationships that could be of personal and professional value. "The wine business puts you in contact with wealthy and powerful people who can introduce you to new opportunities." While he does not divulge the names of his famous clients, they include movie stars, royalty, politicians, and the CEOs of some of the world's best-known companies.

José Manuel also found it appealing that the industry was fragmented and multinational corporations hadn't been able to dominate it. According to José Manuel, "The three or four leading manufacturers of soda, beer, and whisky have 80 percent of the worldwide market. However, even in countries like Australia and Chile, the three or four main wineries represent only a small portion of sales. Independent operations make up the majority of the sector." He felt that the wine industry's fragmentary nature gave him a better chance of leaving something behind for his children. "Generally speaking, only a small percentage of businesses stay in a family's control until the third generation. In the wine industry, there is a much better history of family legacy," he says.

Your reasons for choosing a certain sector in which to start an emerging market business may be completely different from José Manuel's. After all, you may not feel the need to build a legacy or rub shoulders with kings and presidents. The important thing is to know what your priorities are so that you can accurately identify an industry that meets your personal needs. As José Manuel's story shows, this is one of the best ways to ensure your success.

Do Your Research

Although José Manuel learned a great deal about investing while he was at Goldman Sachs and Santander Bank, he had never worked in wine or owned his own company. To make sure he started off on the right foot with O. Fournier, José Manuel first learned all he could about the wine industry. "It was several years between when I started to think about the project and when I purchased the property in Argentina," he says. "I took the time to speak with winery owners in Spain, the U.S., and France. That gave me the opportunity to develop a broad vision for my business."

Despite a lack of knowledge and direct experience, coming from outside an industry does have certain benefits, according to José Manuel. "When you sit down and talk with a family that has been in the wine business for three hundred years, you learn a great deal, but you also realize how a three-hundred-year history can limit one's thinking." Because José Manuel didn't have preconceived ideas about wine making or a legacy to live up to, he had the freedom to do what many others could not or would not. By building wineries in three countries and effectively bridging the gap between the Old World and the New, he created a brand whose wines are known as much for their excellent quality as for their country of origin. "The results speak for themselves," he says. "Sales just keep going up and up."

Having an outsider's perspective on an industry can often be a good thing, but in order to identify opportunities and avoid costly mistakes, it is equally critical to do your research. Fortunately, one of the topics people most like to talk about is themselves. Take advantage of this fact in order to learn as much as you can from those who have experience in the type of business you are contemplating.

Collaborate with the Locals

O. Fournier is one of the most successful and well-known wineries in Mendoza's prestigious Valle de Uco. However, when José Manuel first visited in December 1999, few people outside of Argentina had even heard about the area. "At the time, it wasn't common knowledge that many of Argentina's best wines were being made with grapes from Valle de Uco," he says. "They were like a secret ingredient."

José Manuel discovered the secret and the opportunity to be a pioneer by speaking with his Mendocino friends in the wine business. "When I told them that I was looking for a cold microclimate with a large difference between day and night temperatures, they immediately recommended the valley," he says. At first, José Manuel was skeptical because none of the labels on the Argentine wines he drank mentioned Valle de Uco. However, after visiting the region and seeing for himself that high-quality grapes could indeed be produced on spectacular, low-cost land at the base of the Andes, he became convinced. "The fact that I did not go where many of the larger and better-funded investors built wineries set O. Fournier apart from the competition," he says. "Listening to the advice of people who knew a lot more than I did made all the difference."

The design of the O. Fournier winery, like its location, also came about as the result of collaboration with professionals in Mendoza. The architectural firm of Bormida & Yanzon worked closely with José Manuel's oenologist to produce a radical-looking yet extremely practical production facility. Today, O. Fournier is known not only for spectacular wines but also for its equally spectacular architecture.

Even though many say the winery resembles a Star Wars space-ship parked at the foothills of the Andes, it is highly functional, so that grapes delivered to the top floor of the structure are processed downward via gravity into fermentation tanks.

"I gave the architects complete freedom to design a truly unique facility so long as they didn't interfere with the wine-making process," explains José Manuel. "I didn't want tourists to say, 'It's nice, but it's just another winery.' Going along with what the architects and my winemaker wanted to do was a good bet. Thanks to them, our wines and our winery are unforgettable."

A newcomer to a country as well as an industry can't afford the arrogance of assuming he already knows where to go and what to do. O. Fournier is a success precisely because José Manuel teamed up with top Argentine professionals to help him create something special. "You have to choose good people and then give them the space they need to work," he suggests. Don't forget the importance of collaboration when embarking on *your* emerging market venture.

Be Cautious

José Manuel found that starting a project in an unfamiliar industry in an emerging market was infinitely more complicated than he first imagined. Therefore, he advises finding a balance between ambition and caution: "You must act with great care because, in the end, the details you overlook could be the ones that most affect the outcome of your project." One detail you should not neglect is the human tendency to perceive outsiders as rich, ignorant, and easily fooled.

"Because emerging markets often have chaotic histories of economic and social calamity, their citizens are capable of extreme generosity as well as extreme corruption," says José Manuel. "On one hand, Argentines always make you feel welcome. The warmth of the people surprised me from the very first day I arrived here. On the other hand, employees I supported like a father have betrayed me with lawsuits, and I'm sometimes overcharged because I speak with a Spanish accent." When you are considering a potential partner, employee, or advisor, you must evaluate personal integrity above all else, he insists.

As is the case with many foreign investors in Argentina, José Manuel initially encountered discrimination when he tried to purchase real estate. "When I went to speak with a real estate agent about a plot of land I had seen, he quoted a price that was double what the owner told me only an hour before." Fortunately, the agent had forgotten that the listing was posted in his office window. How did José Manuel handle the deception? "I said to him, 'What you've just described doesn't interest me. The property that does interest me is the one you have in your window that is exactly the same size, exactly the same shape, and in exactly the same location, but for exactly half the price."

José Manuel was so offended when the agent replied that the property had already been sold and he had "forgotten to remove it from the window" that José Manuel decided to close the deal directly with the owner. "I felt like I owed the agent nothing because, when I did the right thing, he tried to cheat me," he says. The real estate agent must have come to the same conclusion; he never asked José Manuel or the property owner for a commission.

Since that day in the real estate agent's office, José Manuel always keeps his mouth shut when he is involved with important business transactions in Argentina. Now, he either sends a local person to represent him or negotiates entirely in writing to avoid having his foreign accent put him at a disadvantage. "Don't try to go it alone in the developing world," he says. "An investment might seem like a good opportunity even at double the fair price; however, your business will be twice as successful if you pay the true market value. Enlist the help of trustworthy advisors to be sure you are getting a fair deal on goods and services."

Price-gouging incidents aside, for José Manuel, employee lawsuits are the most frustrating and disillusioning aspect of doing business in Argentina. "We've had employees sue us for outrageous things and win their cases. People here take advantage of the idiosyncrasies in the labor law in order to gain the upper hand," he says.

José Manuel minimizes labor problems by surrounding himself with trustworthy individuals and maintaining tight control. "I limit employee access to the financial aspects of my company, but it's even more important to be rigorous in the interview process. Dishonest people can always find ways to take advantage of you once they're in the door."

To be sure he doesn't choose badly, José Manuel tries to hire people he already knows or has heard good things about, and he has every job candidate interviewed by at least four other individuals. "Eighty percent of the value of a company is related to the people who work for it, so hiring personnel is the most important business decision an owner makes," he says. At O. Fournier, the process begins with an initial filtering of candidates by the person who will eventually supervise the new hire. Then, all of the company's senior managers interview those who made the short list. "It's fundamental that there is the greatest consensus possible when selecting personnel and that Argentines themselves do most of the interviewing. After all, they have a better feel than I do for who is honest and who is a potential problem," notes José Manuel. In addition to careful screening, he also hires from the area around his winery by announcing openings for midlevel positions on Valle de Uco radio stations. "In nearly all parts of the world I have found people from the countryside to be the most sincere and reliable. They maintain their family values and cultural traditions much better than city dwellers."

Discrimination and dishonesty can make business in emerging markets feel like playing the lottery and cause many to think twice about investing. Nonetheless, if you are aware of and prepared for the pitfalls, you can take measures to avoid them, just as José Manuel does. When you make a major purchase or negotiate the terms of a key agreement, take a trusted, local friend or advisor along with you, or send him or her in your place. When you are considering taking on partners, consultants, or employees, get multiple references and ask several people you trust for their opinions of the person. By doing so, you'll stand a better chance of being treated fairly in transactions and avoiding the few bad apples that can ruin an entire business.

Change Your Investment Mentality

"Many emerging markets are convulsive, so first-world investment parameters and logic don't apply," José Manuel observes. "If you come here with ideas set in stone, this isn't the place for you. You have to start from zero and build your business 'a la Argentina' if you want to succeed."

In part, doing business the Argentine way means financing your venture out of your own pocket. Small-business loans at low interest rates are rarely available from banks. "All the money I ever earned, all the money I ever saved, and all the money I ever borrowed is invested in my company," says José Manuel. "The financial element of business practically doesn't exist in Argentina compared to the U.S. or Europe. Here, it's cash or nothing." To that end, when José Manuel needed capital to complete the first O. Fournier winery, he turned to his family rather than to an Argentine bank. "My father was my first investor," he says. "I've added additional private investors as the project has grown."

According to José Manuel, the lack of financing in emerging markets can actually be a good thing: "As we've recently seen in the U.S. and Europe, leverage is a double-edged sword. Banks are notoriously inflexible partners when you run into problems." Furthermore, he notes, a scarcity of easy money forces entrepreneurs to build financially sound businesses. "Because the personal capital requirements are much higher than in the developed world, you're more focused when you start out. When it's your own money you tend to be careful about how it's spent."

Besides thinking about financing in a different way, José Manuel strongly recommends adopting a new sense of timing when doing business in Argentina. "Decisions about when to buy and when to sell are more critical than back home because the differences between economic peaks and valleys are much greater. If you learn to do things like the locals, you can make a fortune from the huge swings in asset values," he explains. Indeed, the 2001 financial crisis was a tremendous opportunity for the Argentines who had sold out to foreign corporations several years earlier. When the crisis occurred, they repurchased their businesses for a fraction of what they had sold them for.

"In places like Argentina you don't sell so you can retire and go fishing in the Caribbean. You sell so that, in one or two years, you can buy your company back for 20 percent of its peak value and generate substantial wealth for yourself and your family in the process," says José Manuel. "It's not a normal way to think about business, but it's part of the reason why the opportunities are here and not in the developed world."

In North America and Europe entrepreneurs often build companies using venture capital and bank loans with the goal of one day "cashing out" via a sale or an IPO. In emerging markets, many expatriate entrepreneurs build companies using their own money with the goal of creating new lives for themselves in environments that defy traditional economic logic. To prepare for the opportunities that countries like Argentina present, you have to change your investment mentality. As José Manuel says, "You're going to have to move quickly, make hard decisions, and consider the impossible possible."

Incorporate Technology

"Without recent advances in communications technology I wouldn't have been able to build the multinational company I have," says José Manuel, an early adopter who constantly asks himself how the latest technological tools can improve his business. O. Fournier was one of the first wineries in Argentina to develop a website, as well as one of the first to open an online store. "Technology gives you the ability to create businesses that previously didn't even exist. It also generates a superior return on investment."

Before Facebook allowed corporate accounts, José Manuel opened one under his own name and posted news about O. Fournier on it. And when Blackberry phones first came out, he tried to get Skype working on his phone via an Internet connection. The application was blocked, yet that didn't stop him from using the technology at his wineries. "We installed Wi-Fi everywhere," he says. "Not last month, but five years ago." Now nearly everyone in the company uses Skype. "Since we have staff in three different countries, it's an essential tool for staying in contact and keeping communication costs down."

You don't have to be an early adopter or respond to 80 percent of your e-mails within an hour as José Manuel does, but it is a smart bet to incorporate tools such as Skype and Wi-Fi into an emerging market business. They are low-cost solutions that facilitate communication and collaboration on a global scale that was unimaginable or impractical only a few years ago. "The productivity benefits of technology are an absolute certainty," insists José Manuel.

Conclusion
Put Together a Winning Hand

Even though José Manuel says he "jumped into" the wine business, in reality, he took the time to carefully prepare a winning hand for the game he was about to play. First, he thought about his personal objectives and decided that wine making was a good way to reach them. Then he spoke with industry veterans around the world to learn the business and identify potential opportunities. Once his long-term vision was defined, he collaborated with local experts to create wines that are as unique as the facility in which they are produced. Finally, he brought his talented and charming wife on board to ensure that O. Fournier offers tourists a gourmet experience that includes wine *and* food. The entire process actually took more than five years.

To be sure, José Manuel has faced many challenges; including discrimination as a foreigner and being taken advantage of as an employer. However, he has been able to overcome them, he says, through "vision, hard work, a great team, and a good deal of luck." In doing so, he succeeded in his main goal of establishing a legacy for his children; it's a sure bet they won't have to eat frozen Big Macs when they go off to college. "Perhaps they would have preferred a trust fund rather than a winery," he jokes, "but you only live once and it's important to leave something tangible behind."

LESSON 8

Rather than simply playing the cards life deals you, stack the deck in your favor by defining your goals. Then start a business in the emerging market and the industry that offer you the best chance of reaching those goals. To improve your odds of success, be sure to do your industry research and involve a trusted local advisor in critical business transactions.

Spirited Partners

*"We never let any doors slam in our faces. If they did,
we found a solution by going in another direction."*
—LINDSAY DAVIDSON

Lindsay Davidson, born and raised in Houston, Texas, and Emil Balthazar, who grew up in Budapest, Hungary, own and operate one of Mendoza's most unusual small businesses. From a distillery located in Valle de Uco, they produce and export vodka, brandy, and grappa to the United States, Australia, and Europe.

While Emil and Lindsay aren't the only ones in the area making spirits, they do produce the world's only vodka distilled entirely from Malbec grapes. It's called Primo. Emil explains, *"Primo* is a word in English that connotes 'first' or 'best.' In Spanish it means 'cousin.' Since our vodka is the first of its kind and made with the same grapes as wine, Primo seemed like the perfect name."

In addition to striking bottle and label designs, Primo vodka is known for its award-winning quality and special taste. "During our very first year of production we won the Double Gold Award at the San Francisco World Spirit Competition," recalls Lindsay proudly. She has a right to feel good about their achievement. Every judge gave Primo a gold rating in the nonflavored vodka category. Journalist Ian Mount, writing for *Fortune* magazine, observed,

"Primo is the smoothest vodka I've ever tried, smoother even than many of the wines I've so recently sipped."

Raised in a country with many tiny distilleries that produce fruit-based liquors, Emil thought of making spirits long before he visited Argentina. "In New York City I tried and really liked a French vodka called Ciroc that was distilled from Mauzac Blanc and Ugni Blanc grapes. Since there were only four or five vodkas in the world made from grapes, it seemed like a good niche market."

Lindsay had spent ten years in a service-based industry and was looking for the financial security that a successful consumer product could offer. "As a headhunter, my phone was always ringing, but I constantly worried about whether it would ring tomorrow," she explains. Lindsay wanted to be involved in a business that produced something people would buy repeatedly. "Like soap," she says, half joking. "I was thrilled with Emil's concept for a vodka because, when you get older, it's much easier to produce a product than to provide a service." There were other benefits as well. "It's a lot more fun to make vodka than to make soap," quips Emil. Lindsay agrees: "And we have a lot more friends because we do!"

Emil and Lindsay's stories begin continents apart, even though they share similar entrepreneurial backgrounds. After obtaining a degree in journalism from New York University, Lindsay worked her way up the ladder in the magazine industry. She rose from assistant to vice president in charge of circulation at *American Express Travel & Leisure* and *Food & Wine*. In 1999, she founded a headhunting firm focused entirely on major magazine publishers. "It was a logical step for me because I knew the industry, and I knew all the players in it," Lindsay says. Several years later, she started a website that she describes as "a mini Monster.com for the publishing world."

Following his graduation from high school in Budapest, Emil left socialist Hungary in 1985 and immigrated to Canada. He attended the Vancouver Film School and worked as an assistant director on various B movies. In 1990, Emil briefly returned to Budapest "when the socialists became capitalists." There he started his first company—one that sold scratch-and-win lottery tickets. The venture led to a business that manufactured and distributed calling-card dispensing machines in Germany. Later, he moved to New York City, where he ran an antique business and dabbled in the restaurant industry.

Lindsay and Emil met in New York in 2004. In October 2005, the couple decided to take a vacation to Argentina. Initially, they were planning on visiting only Buenos Aires, but they decided it would be a good idea to "get out of the big city and go drink some wine in the foothills of the Andes," as Lindsay puts it. They fell in love with Mendoza instantly. Less than a year later, they were making vodka in their new home.

Despite moving to a foreign country without knowing the difficulties they might encounter, Emil and Lindsay still feel their quick decision to drop everything and relocate to South America produced many great results. "It changed our lives and opened our minds," they say.

Let's take a closer look at their story to learn just how this couple overcame the challenges of doing business in an emerging market in order to create one of the world's most original vodkas.

Find the Right Spot and Go for the Gold

Before they moved to Argentina, Emil and Lindsay had already identified the type of business they wanted to start. That allowed them to define their investment criteria and find the best place in the world to produce Primo—or recognize such a place if they happened to stumble upon it by accident.

To make vodka, a master distiller like Emil Balthazar requires a large quantity of a single raw material, whether it is grapes, grains, or potatoes. "You have to distill at least three or four times to reach an alcohol level of 95 percent," explains Emil. "Each time you do, the percentage of alcohol goes up while the volume of your raw material goes down." As a result, Emil and Lindsay knew they needed to locate their business in a region with an abundance of grapes. Thanks to its unique climate, Mendoza offered a nearly unlimited supply.

"Because the weather is constant, there aren't huge differences in the harvest from one season to the next as there are in Europe. And because the water comes from the Andes' snowmelt, rather than rainfall, there is a reliable high-quality supply," Emil explains. The combination of consistent weather and plentiful water meant that in Mendoza there would always be plenty of grapes with which to make vodka.

Low prices also helped convince Emil and Lindsay that Mendoza was the right location for Primo. "We couldn't afford to go to Sonoma or Napa and do what we wanted to do. Even though there's inflation in Argentina, the price of bottles, labels, capsules, grapes, labor, and land is still far less than back home," says Lindsay. Emil agrees: "Before visiting Argentina, we were talking about California or maybe New Zealand. However, those markets are quite expensive. Starting our business here cost us less than half of what it would have elsewhere."

When Emil and Lindsay were on the plane, returning to New York from their first trip to Mendoza, a lightbulb lit up in their heads. Emil recalls, "All the things we saw and learned by chance from meeting and talking to people on our trip just came together. We said, 'Let's make our vodka in Argentina. There's no shortage of grapes, the climate is great, and it's a lot less expensive than Europe or the States." Within six months, the couple was living in Mendoza. "We just packed up and moved," Lindsay recalls. "We literally went for the gold."

If you are able to define even your most basic investment criteria, it will be easier for you to put two and two together, as Emil and Lindsay did during their travels. Perhaps you don't know exactly what type of product you will produce or what service you will offer. But you should still keep an eye out for places with favorable environments for the industries in which you have experience or that interest you. By doing so, you will be better positioned to recognize and take advantage of opportunities in emerging markets like Argentina.

Capitalize on Regional Strengths

Emil and Lindsay determined that an abundant and reliable supply of grapes and a low-cost operating environment were critical to the success of their venture. That's how they knew they had found what they were looking for and why they moved to Mendoza without hesitation after a brief, unplanned visit. However, it was by lucky accident that they came upon one of the elements most crucial to the success of their business.

Prior to visiting Argentina, the couple knew almost nothing about Malbec. Today, the grape variety is what makes Primo the first and only vodka of its kind. Emil explains, "In the States, there are at least two hundred different brands of vodka. Every week they're coming out with a new flavor, a new this, a new that. But no one else does Malbec. Thanks to our unique ingredient, we are on the way to being really successful." Since 2007, sales of Primo have nearly tripled, from six thousand liters per year to more than fifteen thousand liters in 2010. Lindsay says, "It's like a red carpet has been rolled out for Primo because Malbec is a variety on its way up in the wine world. We're riding a wave similar to the one Chilean wines came in on fifteen years ago. The name, the packaging, the taste, and the Malbec came together like a perfect storm."

Try to incorporate something unique from your new home into your product or service. It could be the very thing that distinguishes your enterprise in the market and gives you a global competitive advantage.

Work as a Team and Go with the Flow

Like other expatriate entrepreneurs, Emil and Lindsay have experienced their share of challenges in Argentina. What frustrates them most, they say, is "standing in line to pay bills, repeatedly returning to government offices to apply for or renew licenses, and carrying around tons of corporate documents in order to do business." To deal with these and other obstacles the couple works as a team. "In the beginning we didn't have a lot of money, so we did everything ourselves. We didn't hire someone to run errands for us," says Emil.

Although Emil and Lindsay never talked about the exact role that each would play, their respective responsibilities "fell into place." Lindsay explains that "we just assumed what we were best at and then filled in the blanks with lawyers, accountants, notaries, etc."

Emil is responsible for everything that needs to be done to get vodka into a bottle. That includes purchasing grapes, distilling, bottling, palletizing, exporting, and shipping. "I'm more of the marketing person, the back end, the numbers," says Lindsay. Despite the division of tasks based on their personal strengths and experiences, Emil and Lindsay collaborated on some of the most important aspects of their business, such as selecting the name Primo and designing the bottle together.

Having grown up in a socialist country, Emil found he was better suited to dealing with long lines and red tape. "Hungary is not much different from Argentina in the sense that it's a lot harder to take care of banking and legal matters than it is in Canada or the States. It's cumbersome because you need to have stamps and certifications for just about everything. Sometimes, it feels like you need a notary to certify your toilet paper just so you can go to the bathroom!"

Lindsay admits that even though Emil often reminded her to think like an Argentine in order to get things done, she still became frustrated. "In the beginning I couldn't help but make comparisons with how business was done back home," she says. "At times, it just seems so inefficient here."

Emil's advice to his partner was to adapt. "You have to be open and just go with the flow," he insists. "Because the environment is different, you must think differently. I'm not saying it's good or bad, but it is different. Adapting is the only way to deal with it."

Even if you don't start an emerging market business with a significant other, be sure to keep in mind the value of teamwork. A partner or an employee can free you up to focus on what you do best. And if he or she is more experienced in a key area, that insight and advice can be of great value.

Learn the Language

The only time during my conversation with Emil and Lindsay when they said exactly the same thing at exactly the same time was when I asked them about the biggest challenge they faced doing business in Argentina. "Speaking Spanish!" was their immediate reply.

From day one, Emil was in charge of turning a historic winery into a distillery and obtaining the corresponding permits. The task was especially difficult for him because he didn't know much Spanish. "Most construction workers and civil servants here don't speak English, so I had to push myself to communicate with them. It took a tremendous amount of effort and concentration to avoid misunderstandings and get things done."

To address their shortcomings with the language, Lindsay and Emil contracted a private tutor. Even so, the learning process wasn't easy. Lindsay explains, "We don't like to study, but after six months here we finally admitted that we needed to improve our Spanish. So we hired a lady to come to our house. At the end of the first lesson, she said, 'Well, you know how to count, and you know all your food groups.' I remember thinking, 'Great! That's all I need to know!'"

A robbery one night at the distillery taught Emil and Lindsay a valuable lesson about how easily misunderstandings can arise when one doesn't speak the local language with fluency. "Some boys jumped over a twelve-foot-high wall and stole our security guard's jacket," Lindsay remembers. "I called the police to tell them in Spanish that we were robbed and they should send help. After I explained the situation there was a long pause on the phone. Then the operator said, 'So, the guard's pants are too small?'"

Lindsay admits that her lack of Spanish puts her at a disadvantage when she is dealing with more important matters than a stolen jacket. "It's frustrating and potentially quite risky if you don't understand every word in a contract or a power of attorney," she says. Based on the difficulties he encountered building the Primo distillery, Emil advises, "Be sure you can speak the language of a country *before* you start doing business there!"

Indeed, it's a mistake to underestimate the importance of language when relocating to a place like Argentina. As we've seen, Emil and Lindsay both ran into problems because they couldn't communicate effectively with the people working with or for them. To avoid misunderstandings, as well as the risk of signing your life away on a contract you don't understand, you must speak the language of your host country. If you don't already have the skill, put it on your to-do list for your new business. Knowing your food groups is fine if you want to order food in a restaurant, but if you want to start a company in an emerging market it's not enough.

Don't Rush to Invest or to Partner

When they moved to Mendoza, Emil and Lindsay made a mistake common among foreign investors. "We purchased one of the first properties we saw that seemed suitable for our offices and distillery. It was a historic winery on a beautiful, tree-lined street," Lindsay recalls. "We didn't care that it required a lot of work because it was so romantic. We fell in love with it like you fall in love with the perfect house. We were so naïve!"

Soon after they made their purchase, the couple realized they were in over their heads. Email says, "It turns out that we backed up to one of the most dangerous neighborhoods in Mendoza. We had to hire twenty-four-hour private security; the guards were constantly calling us in the middle of the night. It was a disaster."

Emil believes one of the main reasons he and Lindsay made such a critical mistake was that they acted too quickly. "We hadn't yet formed relationships with trustworthy people in Mendoza who could advise us. So we ended up buying from individuals who were not forthcoming about the area. They wanted to sell to anybody they could, any way they could."

To avoid problems, Lindsay suggests, "Don't arrive in town and buy an apartment or a house the first week you're there. Get to know the area first, and get a second opinion from a local friend before you purchase." After several tourists were robbed on their way to visit the Primo distillery, Emil and Lindsay decided to move to a safer location. Their business is now located near the town of Tunuyan in Valle de Uco, about eighty-five kilometers (fifty miles) south of Mendoza. "People still comment on how beautiful the old winery was," Lindsay says, "but looks can be deceiving. We were lucky to get out of there before something really bad happened to us, our employees, or our friends."

Emil and Lindsay also moved too quickly to partner with an Argentine distribution company for Primo. "We contracted with a distributor who was 99 percent wine-focused and thus he didn't have the heft to get us on the shelf," remembers Lindsay. "After a year of frustration, we changed to a spirits-based distributor with deep experience in top brands." Sales of Primo not only skyrocketed but became steady. "We saw an 800 percent increase within twelve months of making that change because our new distributor made inroads with retailers and restaurants in Argentina to get the Primo name out there."

When you visit a foreign country for the first time it's easy to be moved by a beautiful landscape, a historic building, a majestic view, or a charming potential partner. Buyer beware! The last people who want you to remove your rose-colored glasses are those with something to sell. To avoid a serious blunder, take the time to perform due diligence. Investigate the pros and cons of a potential investment or future partner and seek the opinion of a third party who knows the local market. Otherwise you could discover, as Emil and Lindsay did, that your dream property is really a nightmare and that your local partner is more of a hindrance than a help.

Join the Expats Community

Soon after they moved to Mendoza, Emil and Lindsay became members of the Mendoza Expats Club. "Some of our best memories from the past five years are the silliness, the laughter, and the camaraderie we've shared with other foreigners living here," Lindsay recalls. Indeed, Emil is still teased at monthly gatherings about his concept to promote Primo by letting a herd of wild elephants run loose in Patagonia. "I drank a lot of wine that day," he remembers with a laugh.

The couple believes that getting together regularly with people who have faced the same challenges they face as newcomers is of great value. "Just sharing stories is a wonderful way to let off steam," they say. Furthermore, a community of fellow entrepreneurs often has knowledge and contacts that can be useful in one's business. When Emil and Lindsay felt their accountant was charging them too much, they asked their expat friends about other options. "Thanks to the people we met through the club we found a great lawyer and a less expensive accountant," says Lindsay. "The organization has been a fantastic resource for us."

Although one moves to a foreign country in part to make friends with the locals, it's essential to associate with expatriates as well. When I was an exchange student in Australia, the program coordinators made sure all participants met once a month in someone's house for food and drinks. For those of us who were having trouble adjusting to life far from home, the gatherings were a godsend. They gave us the opportunity to share our frustrations and discover to our great relief that we were all going through pretty much the same experience. Associating with other foreigners, even of your own nationality, doesn't mean you are "copping out" on life as an expatriate entrepreneur in an emerging market. Rather, it is an essential step in the cultural adaptation process. It also helps you gather information and make contacts that are invaluable to the development of your business. If an expats club exists where you're going, join it. If it doesn't, form one yourself.

Conclusion
Face Challenges with Passion and Tenacity

Emil and Lindsay knew a lot before they arrived in Mendoza, including the type of business they wanted to start and that they worked well together as a team. They both possessed entrepreneurial experience, and Emil had spent years living and working outside his native Hungary. Nonetheless, the couple encountered their fair share of difficulties. For one thing, they became emotionally involved with the purchase of real estate. This clouded their judgment and caused them to rush into a decision without getting a second opinion. In addition, their lack of familiarity with Spanish meant they sometimes had communication problems with employees, partners, and contractors.

What is notable about Emil and Lindsay isn't that they made mistakes in the course of building their company. All entrepreneurs make mistakes, especially when they are starting a business in a foreign environment. What's important is how they overcame their initial missteps to create a unique and award-winning product. "We never let any doors slam in our faces. If they did, we found a solution by going in another direction," Lindsay explains. In other words, be passionate and tenacious as you embark on your new venture. Those traits are keys to survival in an emerging market.

LESSON 9

Vodka must be distilled many times to remove imperfections and produce a drinkable product. Similarly, the secret to success in emerging markets is not a perfect start but rather a good foundation and a commitment to continual improvement. Think about a potential project, find the ideal place for it, and then go for the gold.

10

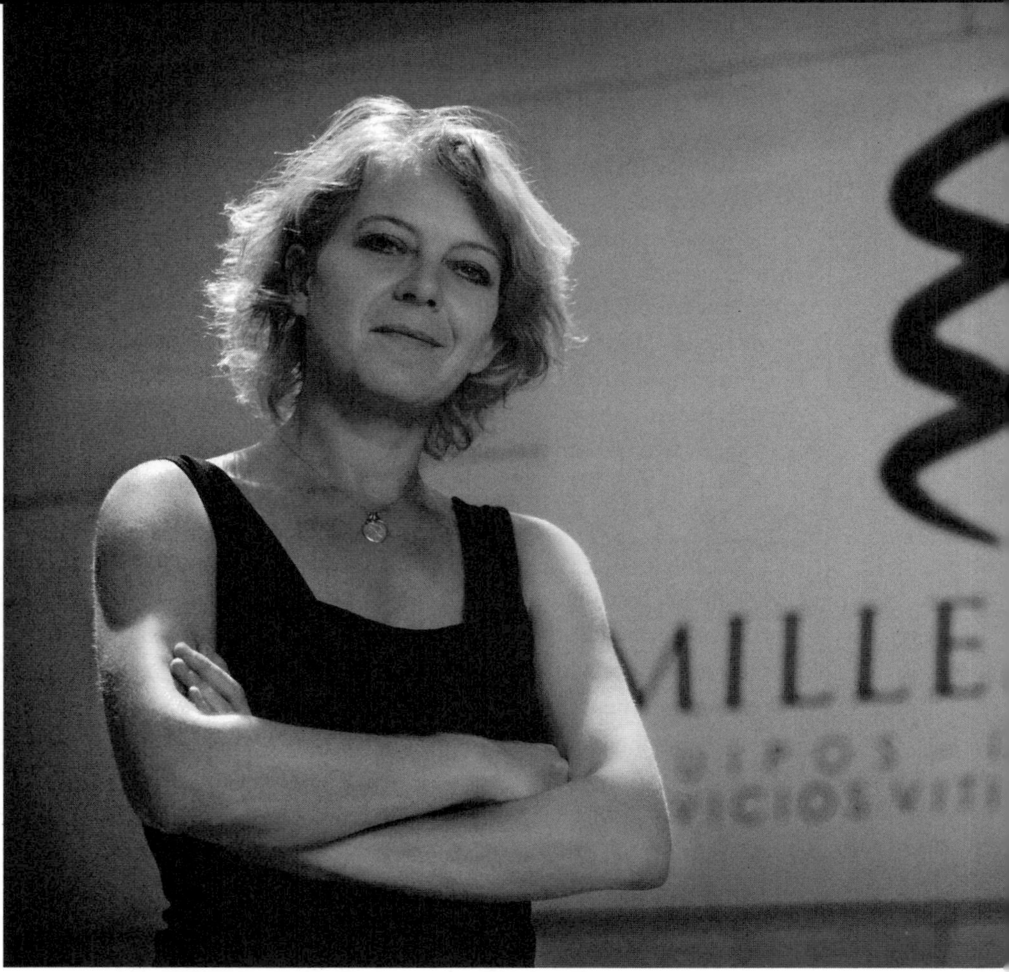

La Franchuta Brava

"You put me in a place, and I do whatever it takes to get things done. That's just my nature."
—HELENE CHEVALIER

At first glance, you wouldn't guess that Helene Chevalier lives up to her reputation as *La Franchuta Brava*, or "The Fierce Frenchie." Tall, blond, and in her early forties, she is a charming conversationalist who easily wins people over with her sharp wit and sense of humor. However, as anyone who has done business with Helene knows, there is tremendous strength hidden under her soft exterior. "My customers call me *La Brava* because I'm persistent and also a firm negotiator," she says. "Sometimes, I get angry and say to them, 'I'm not going to come down even one more cent. These aren't washing machines I'm selling!'"

Indeed, it isn't washing machines that Helene sells. She is the owner of Millesime S.A., a company that imports and distributes European wine-making equipment in Argentina. "We sell presses, pumps, and barrels—all types of machinery for wineries," she explains.

Helene is Parisian by birth, but because of her father's work she spent the first nine years of her life in central Africa in countries including Zaire and Congo. "When you are raised overseas and

135

move around a lot," she observes, "you grow up without feeling connected to a certain place. As a child, people would ask me where I was from, and I wouldn't know what to tell them. I just said, 'I was born in Paris.' But it was for the best. Not having roots gave me the freedom to go many places and do many things in my life."

One example is the year Helene spent in China when she was only twenty. "I was at the university in Canton for three months, and then I traveled all over the country," she remembers. "It was in 1990, right after the Tiananmen massacre, so nobody was speaking about China like they do these days. Living there was something no one else even thought about." In fact, Asia is Helene's first love. "If I weren't in Argentina, I would be running my own business in China or India," she says.

After Helene returned from the Orient, she completed two years of university studies in the humanities and went to work for a French conglomerate that built newspaper printing factories in Eastern Europe and the former Soviet Union. She spent three years in Prague coordinating construction projects in Warsaw, Olomouc, and Moscow. "My job didn't have much to do with China, but it was great experience," she recalls. "I learned a lot about doing business in emerging markets."

In 1995, Helene started her first personal venture. Ironically, it was back in her "native" France. "In Provence I renovated houses with a small group of workmen," she says. "The business was a big success, but after three wonderful years, my partner ran off with all my operating capital. I was ruined." She sums up her initial entrepreneurial experience as "one step forward and one step back."

With no money and nothing to lose, Helene decided to visit her brother, who had a job selling wine-making equipment in Chile. "One afternoon, I met his Spanish and Chilean bosses. Shortly after that meeting, they asked me if I wanted to move to Mendoza to sell their stainless steel tanks in the Argentine market. Of course, I said yes. After all, I had nothing better to do."

So it was that Helene found herself in Argentina in 1999. "I didn't speak Spanish, I didn't have any contacts, I didn't know the industry, and I couldn't tell the difference between a wine press and a destemmer," she remembers. "I had zero experience." To make matters worse, the only help Helene received from her new partners was a hotel room, fifty dollars, and the mission to "start a company."

She spent her first week in Mendoza locked up in her room asking herself, "What am I going to do?" However, she didn't waste time in her self-imposed solitary confinement. "I spent all day every day watching television in order to develop an ear for Spanish," she says. Given that she already spoke Czech, German, English, Chinese, and French, it didn't take her long to pick up the basics of the language.

Once Helene felt comfortable enough to venture out, she immediately got to work setting up her business. "I faced all kinds of obstacles, but at the time, it didn't seem that complicated to me. You put me in a place, and I do whatever it takes to get things done. That's just my nature."

When I questioned Helene about her lack of formal training, she responded, "The basic requirement for everything I do is common sense. Project management and technical service call for the ability to anticipate, to adapt, and to react in a positive way during crisis situations. Nothing more, nothing less."

Helene has come a long way from her early days with little money, one unproven supplier, and no industry experience. Today, she owns a thriving company with twenty employees and represents nearly a dozen European manufacturers. How did she manage to create a business and a life for herself in Argentina out of such humble beginnings?

Change Your Chip

To survive and prosper in a foreign environment, Helene made a "change of chip." That is how she explains the process by which some people adjust to circumstances, as if they are switching out a memory card in a computer. "It's the secret of my success," she insists. "When you are in a strange place and find yourself asking, 'How am I going to deal with this situation?' the trick is to alter your mentality. It's difficult, but it's the best way to adapt and to solve problems."

As an example, Helene tells the story of a European manufacturer that sent a grape press to Argentina—on three separate occasions. "When the first press arrived in Mendoza, it was loaded onto a flatbed truck for its trip to the winery. Unfortunately, the driver didn't realize how tall the press was and rammed it under a bridge. So the president of the winery ordered a second press and told the trucking company to take an alternate route. The driver rammed the second press under a different bridge! When the third press arrived, the president got in his car and personally followed it all the way to the winery. He finally realized that he needed to think of himself as a bridge-spotter in a car rather than a president behind a desk. He changed his chip."

Helene credits her early exposure to Chinese language and culture for her mental flexibility. "I feel at home when I'm in China, especially when it comes to my thought process. I believe that a situation is not necessarily as it initially appears to be. If you are willing to look at it from a different viewpoint, you can better deal with it. That's a very Chinese attitude."

To be clear, Helene says that "changing your chip" has nothing to do with being in a specific country. "I arrived in Argentina by coincidence because an opportunity was given to me. If I had moved to Eastern Europe or Asia, I would have had to change my mentality just the same. No matter where you go in the world, you must mold yourself to the local environment."

In Argentina, one area in which Helene had to modify her thinking was productivity. "Because of the culture, people in Mendoza work many more hours than they would in Europe to achieve the same results. I quickly realized that if I didn't accept the slower pace, I wouldn't survive in this market," she says. These days, *La Brava* scolds foreign investors who are frustrated that it sometimes requires a whole day to accomplish what they could do in two hours back home. "When I see them cursing and complaining about how long it takes to get things done here, I say, 'Stop fighting it, or you'll be gone in less than a year!' You adapt or you fail."

Helene also cautions expatriate entrepreneurs to avoid thinking no change of mentality is required in a country settled by Europeans. "You arrive in Buenos Aires, and you are reminded of Paris. You have a coffee in a sidewalk café, eat a nice steak, and admire the belle époque architecture. Nothing seems exotic. However, Argentines think like Argentines, not Europeans." That's exactly why replacing her European mental chip with an Argentine one has been so critical to Helene's success. "This was a country of immigrants, yet these days, nothing remains of Europe except a façade. There is a tremendous cultural gap, and I changed my thinking accordingly in order to achieve my goals."

Helene Chevalier is proof that changing your mentality, as difficult as it may be, is key to being successful as an expatriate entrepreneur in an emerging market. After all, eleven years ago she started a company in Argentina from zero—and she and her company are still here today. Remember: Cultivating the ability to view business issues from a new perspective can be one of the best ways to avoid obstacles on the road to success in a foreign land.

Educate Your Business Partners

It's not enough for an individual to change her way of thinking to successfully do business in developing countries. Companies must change theirs as well. If you have a business that imports and distributes products, educating overseas suppliers is critically important. Helene explains, "I have to teach European firms how Argentina works because, if they make mistakes with paperwork, I have terrible problems receiving their shipments.

The customs regulations here are unusually complicated and protectionist."

As an example, Helene recounts the story of a French manufacturer that included six bottles of mineral water in a container of high-end equipment bound for Mendoza. "The machinery was absolutely essential to the opening of a brand-new winery, but it got stuck in Buenos Aires for six months just because the water hadn't been declared on a customs form. You can explain all you want that there was no intent to deceive, that the water was a mistake, and that it was clearly not an attempt to smuggle something valuable into the country. But you would be wasting your breath. A tiny error is all the leverage a customs official needs to demand a 'special payment.' "

While many criticize Argentina for its corruption (on Transparency International's 2009 Corruption Index, where the least corrupt country is number 1, Argentina ranked 106th), Helene says it isn't fair for foreign companies to place all the blame at the country's doorstep when they encounter difficulties. "Once you've made a mistake and gotten yourself into a situation, it's pointless to fight the system. You screwed up by not hiring a consultant and not doing things according to the regulations, so you have to accept the consequences."

One of Helene's core services is helping European manufacturers follow the local rules. "I explain that they must detail the origin, weight, composition, and exact value of every single item they ship. When someone complains to me about having to make a list for thousands of parts, I say, 'Okay, don't do it, but the shipment will never enter the country.' My advice is based on what I've learned living here, fighting every day, and making a lot of mistakes in the beginning. It's my added value as a distributor."

Helene demands her suppliers trust her guidance, and usually they do. In fact, it's one of her unwavering conditions. Even though some choose to work with distributors who make things sound easy, by being firm and clear about what it takes to export to Argentina,

La Brava has earned the respect and the loyalty of some of the wine industry's most important manufacturers. It is on that respect and loyalty that she has built a thriving business. As you are starting your own emerging market venture, remember that using your knowledge of local customs can help partners or customers avoid costly mistakes and solidify your business relationships.

Be Prepared to Self-Finance

Following the 2001 Argentine financial crisis, many foreign companies sold out or closed operations altogether when their assets were suddenly devalued and their revenue streams converted from dollars to pesos. It was a wonderful opportunity for expatriate entrepreneurs like Helene who had faith in Argentina and a long-term vision. "Several manufacturers decided they no longer wanted to sell directly in this market, so I offered to hire their technicians and distribute their products myself," she recalls.

That business came at a price, however. Although Helene's new suppliers were willing to let her represent them, they weren't willing to finance her fledgling company in any way. "Obtaining operating capital to pay salaries and ongoing expenses has always been the most challenging aspect of what I do," she says. "When the European companies left, they told me they weren't willing to risk another cent on Argentina. The local banks wouldn't lend me money either. They figured I'd leave sooner or later as well."

Helene's only option was to self-finance. "I had to put all my money back into the company in order to keep my team of experts." It was a good decision. Today, Helene's staff is what sets her apart in the marketplace. "When you are selling in a highly competitive environment, clients put tremendous value on the consistency and quality of technical service. That's why it's so important that the people who started with me ten years ago are still with me today. I wouldn't have survived without them."

In emerging markets where financing options are limited or nonexistent, entrepreneurs often have no choice but to build rock-solid businesses from the start *with their own money*. Once a business has begun to operate, there is little or no credit available with which to prop up a badly performing venture or keep things going until a future break-even point. According to Helene, one of the only ways to obtain capital and cope with challenges like inflation (which has historically been quite high in Argentina as well as in other developing countries) is "to raise prices slightly, while, at the same time, trying to increase sales volume." The day the formula doesn't work is the day that Helene and her peers close their businesses.

Be Fierce

Because Mendoza is a place where personal references are essential to one's professional success, as a newcomer in town Helene had difficulty convincing potential clients to meet with her. "When one of the region's largest wineries announced they were looking for a new equipment supplier, I went to see them," she says. "Since they didn't know who I was, they wouldn't even let me in the door!"

To overcome the challenges associated with being an unknown outsider, Helene developed the persona of *La Franchuta Brava*. On the one hand, playing up her nationality made her stand out in people's minds. "The fact that I am French was a big plus," she says. "Potential clients would talk to me just because they were curious to know who I was and what I was doing in Mendoza." On the other hand, being forceful also gave Helene a competitive advantage. "They call me *La Brava* and say I'm a vicious fighter, but it shows they have accepted me. Here you get respect for being firm and fierce, especially as a woman in a male-dominated industry."

Helene also lands business because she is seen as more committed than her competitors. To illustrate, she tells the story of how she won a contract with a winery in San Rafael, the second largest city in the province of Mendoza. "It was wintertime, and the highway was closed due to ice and snow. I decided to go anyway because I desperately needed clients for my new company," Helene explains. As she was about to start on a 120-kilometer (75-mile) journey across a frozen desert, she was stopped at a police checkpoint. "When the officer told me I couldn't pass, I replied, 'You can't hold me back. I have a sale to make!'" With that, Helene hit the accelerator and headed into an icy oblivion. Even the highway patrol wasn't game to chase her into the storm. "All along the route I saw cars that had crashed and slid off the road," she remembers.

The winery had arranged for Helene and her competitors to make their presentations at the same time, yet Helene arrived to an empty parking lot. "When I knocked on their door, the owners looked at me and asked, 'What are you doing here? The highway is closed!' I replied, 'Yes, it's closed. I came anyway.' They were so impressed, they said, 'We're going to sign with *La Brava*—she's the only one who made it!'"

An aggressive reputation can also produce some amusing moments. At a ceremony in the restaurant Anna Bistró, Helene was to receive the Chevalier de L'Ordre du Merite by the French government in front of 150 of her best friends and customers. "I had no idea what to wear," Helene recalls. She had done such a good job of creating her persona of *La Franchuta Brava* that she found it difficult to step out of it even for a moment. "I was always dressed in boots and jeans. . . . That night when everyone finally saw me in a dress, it was quite a shock—even for me!"

When potential clients wouldn't let Helene in the door, she realized it would take strength of character to overcome their skepticism. Today, the large winery that refused to see Helene Chevalier is now *La Franchuta Brava*'s best customer. You don't have to risk your life in a snowstorm to find success as an entrepreneur in an emerging market, but it certainly helps to be persistent and play up what makes you stand out from the crowd.

Conclusion
It's All About Attitude

Throughout her life, Helene Chevalier has enthusiastically taken on challenges that most people would have found intimidating if not overwhelming.

When many believed China was too dangerous even for a brief visit, she jumped at the chance to spend a whole year there just after the Tiananmen Square massacre. In doing so, she learned something even more valuable than the Chinese language—the importance of looking at a problem from more than one perspective in order to find the ideal solution.

Despite having neither money nor industry experience, Helene said yes when she was offered the opportunity to move to Mendoza and build a company. Starting from scratch taught her how to get things done in Argentina and distinguish herself as a value-added distributor for leading European manufacturers.

When potential clients initially slammed the door in her face, Helene accepted the challenge with gusto. "I said to myself, 'I'm going to get in there and make a sale even if it's the last thing I ever do,'" she remembers. The experience was the impetus for *La Franchuta Brava*, the persona with which Helene has overcome numerous obstacles and literally made a name for herself in the Argentine wine industry.

As many companies were abandoning Argentina during the 2001 financial crisis, Helene expanded her business by using her own funds to hire the talent others had spent the time and money to train but then let go. Ten years later her team is what most sets her apart from the competition.

If there's one thing that Helene's story shows us it's that a great deal can be accomplished with a "can-do" attitude. Instead of giving up whenever she encountered problems, Helene toughened up and moved forward. Do the same and you're sure to reach your goals.

LESSON 10

It takes courage to start a business in an emerging market and strength of character to develop opportunities where others see only obstacles. To succeed, you must be able to view challenges from different perspectives and go after your objectives with determination.

11

Critical Success Factors

When he purchased the land for the popular Anna Bistró restaurant, Jerome Constant learned that doing business in Mendoza is not the same as doing business in Marseille. "The three brothers who owned the property took for granted that the entire transaction would be in cash," he explains. "At no time did anyone even mention the possibility of financing or paying with a wire transfer. Those concepts simply don't exist in the minds of most middle-class Argentines."

To complicate matters, one of the brothers was in a wheelchair and couldn't reach the private room for closings on the second floor of the bank. As a result, Jerome found himself counting out thousands of dollars by hand in the bank's lobby. "While the sellers signed the paperwork, I fumbled to assemble huge stacks of bills on a tiny countertop. Every customer in the bank was watching me and thinking 'What an amateur!'"

When Jerome finally finished stacking the bills, he pushed them across the counter to the brothers. "They flipped through my money in a matter of seconds, hid it in their socks and under the wheelchair, and then vanished out into the city as if they had just done a drug deal. For us Europeans, paying for real estate with mountains of cash is something only seen in movies. In Argentina, it's normal."

■ ■ ■

Jerome's experience illustrates the type of challenges a person from the developed world can face in an emerging market. If you start a business in a cash economy, you'd better be prepared to self-finance your project and to count wads of cash quickly and accurately. "It takes practice to learn how to stack bills by positioning and folding them rapidly with your fingers. If you can't do it," Jerome explains, "then you lack one of the most basic requirements for doing business in the land of the gaucho."

In places where the rules are just plain different, expatriate entrepreneurs must take special steps to survive and prosper. Some, such as speaking the local language, setting realistic expectations, and adapting to the native culture (including financial and legal practices), are relevant to success in nearly all foreign environments. Others, such as overcoming bureaucratic obstacles, choosing an industry with minimal government intervention, and buying during an economic down cycle, are especially important to success in emerging markets like Argentina. And still others, such as performing due diligence, seeking advice, and hiring good people, are fundamental to success just about anywhere. Together, they represent the critical success factors for expatriate entrepreneurs in emerging markets. Unfortunately, many entrepreneurs do not adhere to them despite how obvious they may seem to an observer.

During my time in Argentina I've seen executives and entrepreneurs from overseas make mistakes that would be unthinkable back home. They buy the first property they see, partner with the first friend they make, or hire the first person they interview. And they blindly put their trust in locals without performing background checks or carefully analyzing the investment opportunities they're offered with the help of independent experts.[1] Why is this?

---

1. For an example of the timelessness of this phenomenon see *Out of Africa*, Karen Blixen's account of her experiences as an expatriate entrepreneur in Kenya during the early twentieth century. Despite being an extremely well educated person from the Danish aristocracy, Blixen purchased a coffee plantation that by her own account was "too high up" for coffee and spent seventeen years (as well as all of her investors' money) in a hopeless battle against frost, drought, and low yields. Modern-day investors who buy vineyards in Argentina without professional guidance often find themselves battling exactly the same challenges.

As athletes know, in situations of extreme uncertainty or stress, that which comes naturally through years of training suddenly becomes difficult. The phenomenon is commonly referred to as "choking" and is technically defined as the failure of normally expert skill under pressure. Ask a tennis pro to play a televised championship game on a court two-thirds the normal size and she starts to hit like an amateur. Ask one of California's most successful companies to do business in Mendoza and it ends up with waterless vineyard land, employees who embezzle funds, and a winery where waste water runs out toward the walls rather than down into the drains.

Thus it should come as no surprise that executives and entrepreneurs choke just like athletes when they find themselves in unfamiliar circumstances. After all, coping with a foreign language and culture, as well as institutional voids and bureaucracy, can be extremely stressful! What's remarkable about the people in this book is that they did *not* choke. And while the success factors most common to their stories may not be 100 percent comprehensive or applicable to all entrepreneurs, they are indeed revealing. As detailed here, they offer practical guidance on what it takes for someone from North America or Europe to start a business in an emerging market.[2]

---

2. A success factor in and of itself is not a good indication of what it takes to succeed as an entrepreneur in an emerging market. After all, many expatriates had perfect timing when they started a business in an untapped niche market in Argentina immediately after the 2001 financial crisis—and failed just the same because they lacked adaptability or some other factor. The stories in this book demonstrate that it is the *combination* of many factors that is key to success and what differentiates the entrepreneurs I interviewed from their peers who are unsuccessful or plagued with problems.

A Relevant Background

Possessing knowledge, skills, and experiences that can be leveraged for success in a new business and new environment

"It takes previous education and skill to start a business in Argentina."

—CAROLYN GALLAGHER
Uncorking Argentina

Michael Evans hadn't run a tasting room or a private vineyard development, but his experience in politics taught him how to manage teams of people and meet deadlines. Charlie O'Malley, founder of the *Wine Republic* magazine and Trout & Wine tours, had never published a magazine or organized wine tours, but he was a gifted writer with experience escorting French school groups to Ireland. José Manuel Ortega Fournier hadn't managed a winery, but at Goldman Sachs he acquired a work ethic that gave him a competitive advantage in any industry. These entrepreneurs were successful in part because they had the training, work experience, and talent to take advantage of the opportunities they discovered in Argentina. And those who lacked knowledge relevant to the business they were contemplating took steps to address their shortcomings. Carolyn Gallagher returned to California to "take classes, read books, and do research" before starting her tour company. Jerome Constant took measurements in the kitchens and studied the operations of restaurants in Paris before opening Anna Bistró. And Emil Balthazar volunteered as an apprentice at distilleries in Hungary and Germany before launching Primo vodka. The stories in this book demonstrate that preparation as well as one's personal background play a significant role in the success of an emerging market business.

Previous International Experience

Knowing what it is like to live in a foreign environment so as to be prepared for the daily challenges that an emerging market presents

"New markets appear suddenly and then quickly disappear. You have to have the capacity to see opportunities and reinvent yourself and your business accordingly. Those are skills you learn by traveling and by living in the developing world."

—ANNE-CAROLINE BIANCHERI
Caviar Bleu

With the exception of Michael Evans, cofounder of The Vines of Mendoza, and Lindsay Davidson, cofounder of Primo vodka, every person I interviewed spent at least a year overseas before starting his or her own company in Argentina. (To make up for this shortcoming, Michael and Lindsay both partnered with people who had grown up in emerging markets and lived outside their native countries for extended periods of time.) Clearly, going on an exchange program, participating in a volunteer mission, or studying abroad helps one develop the intercultural skills that are vital to success as an expatriate entrepreneur in an emerging market. Gustavo Espitia, owner of Aguamiel hotel, provided particularly good insight into the value of international experience when he told me, "You have to live abroad to open your horizons. I grew up in Mexico thinking that I was really international. Ha! I had no idea. Not until you leave your hometown do you realize how hometown you really are." There is simply no substitute for having lived in a foreign culture and having had to respond on a daily basis to ways of thinking and to situations that you would never encounter back home.

An Entrepreneurial Spirit

The drive to take risks and make sacrifices to satisfy one's need for self-made success

"There are a lot of people in the States who, until recently, felt like they had safe jobs and safe mortgages. These days, what isn't risky?"

—MICHAEL EVANS
The Vines of Mendoza

Jerome Constant, owner of Anna Bistró, had dreamed of running his own business since he was eighteen. When he was just twenty-one, Michael Evans moved to Arizona to start his first company. Straight out of college, tour operator Carolyn Gallagher worked as a teacher and a river guide, never wanting to be an employee in a large company. And Anne-Caroline Biancheri started Caviar Bleu publishing when she was only twenty-three. As a group, expatriate entrepreneurs in emerging markets are born risk takers who thrive in volatile environments. And they often sacrifice personal as well as financial comfort in order to reach their goals. Carolyn Gallagher summed up the entrepreneurial spirit when she said, "In the end, the happier person is the one who takes a risk and rafts down the river. She's not the one who stays on the shoreline observing the water."

Strong Motivation

Wanting to live and work in an emerging market for the right reasons

"The profile of most expats running their own businesses in Mendoza is similar to my own. Coming here doesn't have anything to do with a need to escape from home or make money. It has everything to do with personal development and achieving lifelong goals."

—GUSTAVO
ESPITIA
Aguamiel hotel

Starting a company in a place like Argentina sounds romantic, but something that guidebooks, real estate agents, and travel writers don't often mention is that it is *hard work*. To overcome challenges like red tape and culture shock, entrepreneurs must be driven by something meaningful. Not a single person I interviewed said they moved to Argentina because they wanted to strike it rich or because they were sick and tired of their country's politics. They did so first and foremost because of the tremendous potential for personal and professional growth they saw "on the frontier." And many, like magazine publisher Charlie O'Malley, restaurateur Jerome Constant, tour operator Carolyn Gallagher, and winemaker José Manuel Ortega Fournier, were inspired by lifelong dreams of owning their own businesses in a foreign land. As Emil Balthazar, cofounder of Primo vodka, says, "Lindsay and I are passionate about what we do. *That* is what pushes us further and further along."

Adaptability

Willingness to modify one's expectations and way of doing business according to the cultural context

"I arrived in Argentina by coincidence because an opportunity was given to me. If I had moved to Eastern Europe or Asia, I would have had to change my mentality just the same. No matter where you go in the world, you must mold yourself to the local environment."

—HELENE CHEVALIER
Millesime S.A.

If you come here with ideas set in stone, this isn't the place for you. You have to start from zero and build your business 'a la Argentina' if you want to succeed," says José Manuel Ortega Fournier. Assuming you can succeed as an entrepreneur in an emerging market without changing your mindset and behavior is as foolish as thinking oncoming cars will stop for you at a pedestrian crosswalk in Argentina. Instead of complaining that the locals do things differently than they're done back home, the entrepreneurs in this book reset their expectations and plan accordingly. Jerome Constant orders supplies for Anna Bistró weeks before he actually needs them. "You have to take into account that when you ask for something to be delivered in January, it's sure to arrive in March or April," he notes. "Nobody is going to apologize or admit that it should have been delivered in January." At The Vines of Mendoza, Michael Evans plans ambitious projects but he doesn't expect miracles. "No one is going to work on a Sunday. They are all going to be at lunch with the family," he explains. And Charlie O'Malley makes backup plans in case one of his Trout & Wine tour groups arrives at a winery that has closed for the day without notice. "When I first started my tour business I learned very quickly to hope for the best yet plan for the worst," he says. "I always had a Plan B, C, and D!"

Language Fluency

Speaking the country's native language in order to integrate with and gain respect from the locals as well as to communicate effectively with clients, employees, and suppliers

"Most construction workers and civil servants here don't speak English, so I had to push myself to communicate with them. It took a tremendous amount of effort and concentration to avoid misunderstandings and get things done."

—EMIL
BALTHAZAR
Primo vodka

Every entrepreneur I interviewed mentioned the overwhelming importance of speaking the language of the country in which they live and work. Some, like Lindsay Davidson, had to learn the hard way that knowing your numbers and your food groups isn't enough. When she called in a robbery at the Primo vodka distillery, the police thought she was telling them that her security guard's pants were too small. Other entrepreneurs, like Charlie O'Malley, knew they lacked an ear for language but realized it was better to speak Spanish with a thick accent than to speak no Spanish at all. Emil Balthazar best summed up the advice this group of entrepreneurs had for aspiring entrepreneurs who aren't yet bilingual: "Be sure you can speak the language of a country *before* you start doing business there!" Indeed, the ideal is to learn in advance. But if you are ready to move forward and don't speak fluently, make language study an irrevocable part of your business plan. The people in this book took immersion courses, hired private tutors, or traveled extensively in Spanish-speaking countries in order to perfect their language skills.

Cultural Sensitivity

Recognizing that business is done differently than it's done back home despite superficial similarities in architecture, language, or culture

"You arrive in Buenos Aires, and you are reminded of Paris. You have a coffee in a sidewalk café, eat a nice steak, and admire the belle époque architecture. Nothing seems exotic. However, Argentines think like Argentines, not Europeans."

—HELENE CHEVALIER
Millesime S.A.

"Don't allow yourself to be fooled by sidewalk cafés and fancy Italian suits," warns Anne-Caroline Biancheri. Especially in the case of the European expatriate entrepreneurs I interviewed, success depended in part on recognizing that Argentines are a unique people with a unique culture. Anne-Caroline discovered it took three months to set up a company in Buenos Aires despite the popular saying that "Argentines are Italians who speak Spanish, think that they're French, and act as if they're English." José Manuel Ortega Fournier, a native of Spain, found he had to be just as careful with real estate agents as did Michael Evans, from the United States, even though he speaks perfect Spanish. And Helene Chevalier realized that she needed to replace her European mental "chip" with an Argentine one when she observed that "because of the culture, people in Mendoza work many more hours than they would in Europe to achieve the same results." The entrepreneurs in this book learned to see the Argentines as they really are and not as they wish or expect them to be based on outward appearances. That has allowed them to establish realistic expectations and make plans based on the reality behind the European façade.

A Different Perspective

Leveraging one's uniqueness to identify niche markets that locals may not see and to open doors to business opportunities that might otherwise be closed

"In Argentina, foreigners really stand out. You may be a nobody back home, but, here, it's like, 'Wow!' You're special. And for no reason other than that you speak with a funny accent."

—GUSTAVO ESPITIA
Aguamiel hotel

Jerome Constant could have been speaking for nearly everyone I interviewed when he told me, "The main reason I've been successful here is that I'm different from everyone else, and so is my business." On the one hand, being different helped the entrepreneurs in this book get traction when they were just starting out. For example, Helene Chevalier told me, "The fact that I am French was a big plus. Potential clients would talk to me just because they were curious to know who I was and what I was doing in Mendoza." On the other hand, being different enabled them to perceive needs not visible to locals and address them using skills they had learned in other cultures and industries. Anne-Caroline Biancheri, who publishes the only coffee-table book on Mendoza, says, "If you fulfill an unmet need and you do it well, success is a sure thing." Gustavo Espitia built Mendoza's first hotel for green-conscious tourists. Charlie O'Malley launched the region's only magazine for native English speakers. And Michael Evans opened the first tasting room for wine enthusiasts. It is not by coincidence that the majority of these entrepreneurs' customers are foreigners. Their unique perspectives as outsiders enabled them to target specific clientele with specific unmet expectations and thereby build businesses with a competitive advantage.

Good Timing

Starting a business when costs are low, competition is sparse, and growth is all but assured

"If the 2001 crisis in Argentina hadn't happened, I wouldn't be here."

—JEROME CONSTANT
Anna Bistró

Over and over again the entrepreneurs I spoke with told me that a good sense of timing played a major role in the success of their ventures. Nearly all of them moved to Argentina soon after the country's 2001 financial crisis. Gustavo Espitia's comments were typical of most: "In Mexico, I wouldn't have been able to start a project like Aguamiel. Because Mexico's more economically stable than Argentina, it's much more expensive to do business there. I never would have had the money." It is not by coincidence that nine of the ten people I interviewed built thriving businesses from the ashes of one of the world's largest economic meltdowns. By investing when their dollars or euros had maximum purchasing power, they were able to get started for less, minimize their overall risk, and avoid taking on loans or outside investors. This allowed them to take longer to reach the break-even point, lose less of their nest egg if their businesses failed, and operate without interference or restrictions from third parties. Also, by recognizing early on Argentina's untapped potential in wine and tourism, the entrepreneurs in these pages positioned themselves to be a part of the inevitable boom in those industries as a result of the peso's devaluation.

Flexibility

Changing business plans as conditions change

"When you create a ten-year plan, you have to take into account that you are likely going to have to shift your focus to a different market, redesign your products, or do something completely new. Although business planning is important, it's not as relevant as in the past, because these days change is constant, and markets are increasingly fragmented."

—ANNE-
CAROLINE
BIANCHERI
Caviar Bleu

Thanks to high inflation, fluctuating exchange rates, and constantly changing laws, it's a challenge to meticulously plan the growth of a business in countries like Argentina. "The environment here is so volatile that you can throw out any numbers you like, but in the end, they don't really matter," says Gustavo Espitia. To deal with volatility, the people I interviewed headed in a specific direction with their endeavors but remained flexible enough so that they could make adjustments when unforeseen circumstances arose. Lindsay Davidson and Emil Balthazar moved their distillery to a new location when they realized they had set up shop in a high-crime area. Anne-Caroline Biancheri opened a subsidiary in Santiago, Chile, and published *Santiago Cinco Estrellas* herself when her partner backed out of the project at the last minute. And when several European firms left Argentina after the 2001 economic crisis, Helene Chevalier hired their technicians and distributed their products herself. In short, the stories in this book are proof that being flexible is essential to staying on course toward success in emerging markets.

An Emphasis on Growth

Taking advantage of opportunities as they arise so as to make the most of untapped niches and secure an early competitive advantage

"A big part of our success has to do with the fact that we never stop pushing to extend the brand and grow the business."

—MICHAEL EVANS
The Vines of Mendoza

The previous ten chapters demonstrate the importance of making the most of the opportunities that arise frequently in emerging markets, to ensure the long-term success of a business and establish a competitive position before a market matures. Jerome Constant patiently waited to find a motivated seller in his neighborhood and then purchased another piece of land just down the block from Anna Bistró. He is now building Mendoza's first French bakery on the property. Charlie O'Malley used his *Wine Republic* magazine to quickly and inexpensively test the popularity of new business concepts. Now he has a thriving tour company in addition to his publishing venture. Michael Evans has been expanding The Vines of Mendoza almost from the day he founded it. As soon as his wine-tasting room was open he began working on a private vineyard development (both were the first of their kind in Mendoza). Not long after, he and his partner opened a wine store in the Park Hyatt Mendoza. Once their businesses are up and running, expatriate entrepreneurs in emerging markets don't rest on their laurels. They stay alert to opportunities to start another business, create a product for a new market segment, or expand on what they are already doing. With one win under their belts, it is just that much easier to score a second home run.

Technological Savvy

Leveraging the latest technological tools to inexpensively reach a global market and increase business efficiency

"I wouldn't exist without the Internet."

—CAROLYN GALLAGHER
Uncorking Argentina

Technology has become so important to business in emerging markets that it is a theme in most of the preceding chapters. The Internet allows Charlie O'Malley and Carolyn Gallagher to sell their wine tours online, Gustavo Espitia to fill his empty hotel rooms with last-minute online auctions, and José Manuel Ortega Fournier to monitor in real time the status of his wine fermentation tanks in three different countries. A touch-screen ordering system helps Jerome Constant minimize errors, reduce theft, and improve service in his restaurant. Skype enables Michael Evans to communicate inexpensively with customers around the globe. "Before, voice communication would've cost us a fortune with all the international phone calls we make. These days it essentially costs nothing," he says. In emerging markets far from customers or suppliers, successful expatriate entrepreneurs leverage the latest technological tools to create highly efficient businesses with global reach.

Skill at Cutting Red Tape

The ability to overcome bureaucratic obstacles

"It's a lot harder to take care of banking and legal matters here than it is in Canada or the States. It's cumbersome because you need to have stamps and certifications for just about every-thing. Sometimes, it feels like you need a notary to certify your toilet paper just so you can go to the bathroom!"

—EMIL
BALTHAZAR
Primo vodka

Whether they are forming a company, buying a property, obtaining an operating permit, or opening a bank account, expatriate entrepreneurs in emerging markets usually face more red tape than they would in the developed world—and are good at cutting through it. Charlie O'Malley dealt with bureaucracy using creativity. When he first started out, he wasn't registered as a tourism agency, but he operated as one anyway. "I just paid someone else for his registration number and put it on the sign," he says. Jerome Constant, owner of Anna Bistró, was simply persistent. He told me, "Every time [the bureaucrats] told me I had to return with more documents, I got them and came running back immediately. They couldn't believe it!" And Carolyn Gallagher turned to experts when she felt overwhelmed by banking regulations. "The secret to avoiding headaches is putting together a great team that knows the bureaucratic pitfalls and can help you navigate around them," she says. The experiences of these entrepreneurs demon-strate that the ability to deal with bureaucracy is a requirement for doing business in emerging mar-kets like Argentina.

Skill at Dealing with the State

Avoiding government intervention's negative effects when possible and finding creative solutions when it is not possible

"I feel inflation myself when I buy groceries or eat out, so I know what my employees are going through. My challenge is passing on a 30 percent increase in salaries to the price of a grape press or oak barrel.

—HELENE CHEVALIER
Millesime S.A.

The people in this book are successful in part because they chose not to start businesses in industries in which the Argentine federal government heavily intervenes, such as grain and cattle (where high export tariffs have at times wreaked havoc). They also found ways to cope with the inflation and tight monetary control that are the results of current government policy. To combat the effects of inflation, Helene Chevalier slightly raises the prices of the wine-making equipment she sells while, at the same time, trying to increase sales volume. To counter strict banking regulations (which make it difficult for foreigners to open bank accounts, start companies, and receive wire transfers from overseas), many of the entrepreneurs I interviewed deal in cash, transfer funds via Western Union and currency exchange houses, and receive payment for goods and services via credit card and PayPal. Their stories are evidence that when the state wields tremendous power over certain industries and certain aspects of the economy, success depends on finding ways to work around the policies that discourage entrepreneurship.

A Focus on People

Building close relationships with those who are most important to the growth of a business

"Because it makes me feel good to look after other human beings, I give my customers that extra bit of service they deserve. That's what sets me apart from the other tour operators."

—CAROLYN GALLAGHER
Uncorking Argentina

Building close relationships with employees, partners, and customers was especially important to the entrepreneurs in this book. In many ways, their focus on the human side of business is what sets them apart from other expatriates I know who either came to Argentina and failed or are still here but plagued by constant problems and a bad reputation. Jerome Constant is representative of his successful peers when he says, "One of the reasons I got into the restaurant business was that it gave me the chance to help men and women develop themselves in a positive work environment. It's really gratifying to have that kind of impact in the community." Especially in industries and in cultures where personal relationships are valued above all else, a focus on people is essential for long-term success.

An Eye for Talent

Building teams or forming partnerships that minimize rather than increase the risks of doing business in an emerging market

"The main reason I have been able to overcome the challenges of doing business here is that from the beginning I had a great local partner in Pablo. None of this would be possible without him."

—MICHAEL EVANS
The Vines of Mendoza

Almost without exception, the individuals I interviewed told me that their Argentine partners or employees were key to reaching their goals. In a country where animosity between labor and management is practically institutionalized and many partnerships end in lawsuits, their comments are particularly insightful. They demonstrate that successful expatriate entrepreneurs are good at spotting talent and forming long-lasting and mutually beneficial relationships with quality people. These entrepreneurs do not rush to hire the first person who speaks English or partner with the first friendly local they meet. Instead, people like José Manuel Ortega Fournier proceed with caution and carefully choose with whom they associate. They do so by taking their time to get to know the locals, learning what a job candidate's reputation is in the community, and interviewing many people before making a decision.

An Ear for Advice

Admitting that certain pitfalls in an emerging market can be seen only by people with more knowledge and experience

"You have to be extremely careful when you are doing business in the developing world. If you want to successfully invest in real estate, agriculture, or almost any other sector, it's essential to get good advice. You can't cut corners."

—JEROME CONSTANT
Anna Bistró

Not every entrepreneur I spoke with had an ear for advice when he or she first started doing business in Argentina, but those who didn't quickly developed one after making painful mistakes. Jerome Constant lost the opportunity to buy the first plot of land he found for Anna Bistró because he couldn't get his money into Argentina fast enough to close the deal. "That lot is now worth more than ten times what I would have paid for it," he laments. "By not hiring a consultant for a few thousand dollars, I lost several hundred thousand." Due to a lack of professional guidance, Helene Chevalier also made mistakes when starting out. "I didn't realize that a lawyer was so important to the life of a company here," she says. "So I signed invalid contracts without even knowing it!" Today, Helene credits her attorney for keeping her out of trouble. "He is a great friend and a tremendous help to my business." None of the people in the previous chapters now thinks he or she "knows it all" and can do everything without help in Argentina. These entrepreneurs are successful in large part because they are willing to pay for and listen to the advice of others. Michael Evans's attitude is typical: "Contrary to a lot of entrepreneurs I know back home, I'm happy *not* to be the smartest person in the room. I may want to know how to make wine, but I'm not going to try to figure it out on my own just to save a buck. That's a recipe for disaster. I gladly pay experts for their expertise."

A Personally Rewarding Business

Enjoying one's work to such an extent that the stress of doing business in an emerging market is worth the effort

"Going out to the vineyard and making wine with grapes we planted in raw land five years ago makes every bit of the six and a half days a week I work worth it. At the end of the day, I wouldn't work this hard if I didn't love it. That's what drives me. I don't get up and think, 'Oh no, I've got to work today.' I never feel that way."

—MICHAEL EVANS
The Vines of Mendoza

Duffy Crane, chief operating officer of The Vines of Mendoza, once told me, "The challenge in Argentina isn't the lack of opportunities; it's the deluge of them. You have to carefully choose which ones to go after." Just because an opportunity exists to start an English-language magazine, a wine-tasting room, a private vineyard estate, a vodka distillery, or a French bistro, it doesn't necessarily mean it should be pursued. Charlie O'Malley and José Manuel Ortega Fournier are both highly successful entrepreneurs, but neither could run the other's business. Charlie would be as miserable managing a winery as José Manuel would be publishing a magazine, and both would likely fail as a result. Most of the people in this book didn't jump at opportunities just because they were there. They thought carefully about what they most enjoyed doing and then started a business related to that interest. Especially in places where running a company is made all the more difficult by an unfamiliar and volatile environment, liking one's work is fundamental to success.

A Personally Rewarding Environment

Enjoying one's surroundings and lifestyle to such an extent that it is worth the effort required to create a successful business

"To be happy and have the energy being an entrepreneur requires, you have to be in an environment you like and that agrees with you. You can have a complete commercial success, but if you're not content, and you don't like where you are, what's the point?"

—JEROME CONSTANT
Anna Bistró

Beautiful scenery, friendly people, and a sunny climate do not necessarily mean a country is ideally suited to a certain business. Similarly, an abundance of business opportunities does not necessarily mean that a particular country is ideally suited to a certain person. The entrepreneurs I spoke with chose to invest in Argentina not only because of the low-cost operating environment and the business potential they identified but also because of their love for the country and its people. Helene Chevalier told me, "I'm not here because of my business in and of itself. It's Argentina that I like. You never know what the next day will bring—what type of problem, of prospect, of creative person who wants to do something new." Helene and her peers also value Argentina's pro-family culture. Nearly everyone in this book has started a family since moving here. In conclusion, their stories are proof that being in the right place professionally *and* personally is critical to one's success.

Final Thoughts

When I started writing *Expatriate Entrepreneurs in Emerging Markets* I had certain preconceptions. I thought I'd be talking with individuals who started a business overseas because they were reinventing themselves after a layoff, a divorce, or some other personal calamity. Instead, I discovered that the people I interviewed weren't fleeing or recovering *from* something but rather running *toward* an opportunity—often, to realize a lifelong dream.

I also assumed that as a group, expatriate entrepreneurs in emerging markets would be extremely diverse. Although I found that to be true in terms of their personal histories, nationalities, and work experience, it wasn't true in terms of their approaches to starting a business. I was surprised to learn that these entrepreneurs all listed pretty much the same reasons for their success. There was not a significant difference of opinion on a single point.

Initially, I thought the stories in *Expatriate Entrepreneurs in Emerging Markets* would reveal many lessons specific to running a business in Argentina. However, the individuals I interviewed told me they achieved their goals not only by cutting through this country's red tape and seeing through its European façade but also by adapting to the local environment, filling niches, and hiring good people. In fact, the *majority* of what they said was applicable to expatriates doing business in *any* emerging market.

When my Argentine friends heard about my project, they too had certain preconceptions. Many thought the foreigners I interviewed would sharply criticize this country, its people, and its culture. Although they did mention challenges like bureaucracy, discrimination, and inflation, the people in this book were adamant that the good things outweigh the bad here—and what they most like about living in Argentina are the Argentines. I fully agree with them, but I expected to hear that from two or three people, not the vast majority.

When my expat friends learned about this project, many warned me to not give away all my "trade secrets." They assumed that by telling other expatriate entrepreneurs' success stories I would somehow be putting myself out of business as a consultant. So it was personally rewarding when the people in this book repeatedly told me, without any prompting on my part, that a willingness to listen to advice had been fundamentally important to their success. They know that entrepreneurs don't need access to secret information in order to reach their goals. Instead, they just need to open their ears to people who know more about a certain subject than they do, whether they are friends, employees, business partners, or consultants. As the saying goes, "Half of being smart is recognizing what you are dumb at."

Still other individuals believed I would write a tell-all novel set in Mendoza, where winemakers, con artists, and playboys do business and make love amongst Malbec vineyards at the foothills of the Andes. After all, *"Pueblo chico, infierno grande"* ("Small town, big soap opera"). But this book was never going to be about *that* kind of passion. Instead, I chose to focus on the positive aspects of people's lives and examine how they were able to reach their personal and professional goals within the context of an emerging market. In doing so, I learned that the drama behind the scenes in a community of more than three hundred expatriates isn't nearly as compelling as a handful of success stories (but I'll still put the spicy stuff in my screenplay for the film *Sideways in Mendoza!*).

During the process of writing *Expatriate Entrepreneurs in Emerging Markets*, I also discovered that the words from Ralph Waldo Emerson's "Self-Reliance" are as relevant today as they were when he penned them 170 years ago. He wrote:

If our young men miscarry in their first enterprises, they lose all heart. If the young merchant fails, men say he is ruined. If the finest genius studies at one of our colleges, and is not installed in an office within one year afterwards in the cities or suburbs of Boston or New York, it seems to his friends and to himself that he is right in being disheartened, and in complaining the rest of his life. A sturdy lad from New Hampshire or Vermont, who in turn tries all the professions, who teams it, farms it, peddles, keeps a school, preaches, edits a newspaper, goes to Congress, buys a township, and so forth, in successive years, and always, like a cat, falls on his feet, is worth a hundred of these city dolls. He walks abreast with his days, and feels no shame in not "studying a profession," for he does not postpone his life, but lives already. He has not one chance, but a hundred chances.

His words are different, but winery owner José Manuel Ortega Fournier expressed a similar sentiment to Emerson's when he told me: "If you have a significant capacity for metamorphosis and the ability to fall and get back up, then you have as good a chance of success as an entrepreneur as any MBA student." In short, the people from around the world who start businesses in emerging markets today are the contemporary equivalents of Emerson's "sturdy lads from New Hampshire or Vermont." They are highly motivated and resilient individuals who are not bound to their fate by culture or custom. If the thought of starting a business in a country like Argentina has flashed across your mind, have the courage to take the necessary steps to develop it even if others try to dissuade you. The stories in this book and the lessons they teach us—like Ralph Waldo Emerson and José Manuel Ortega Fournier's words—are evidence that if you have a truly self-reliant spirit, and adhere to a combination of critical success factors, you will surely succeed.

Acknowledgments

Candid feedback from a number of friends and colleagues was essential to the creation of this book. I am particularly grateful to those individuals who invested their valuable time in reading drafts of *Expatriate Entrepreneurs in Emerging Markets* and providing detailed suggestions for improvement, including Arnold Bock, Steven English, Richard Fisher, Deborah Montieth, Ian Mount, Joy Phillips, William Sandy, and the entrepreneurs themselves. Bobbi Linkemer and Ellen Hoffman, both accomplished writers, were invaluable to me as subject matter editors. So was Katherine Pickett as my copy editor and Leticia Rodriguez as my transcriber. Without their professional assistance, this book simply wouldn't exist. Thanks are also in order to my longtime photographer, Federico Garcia, as well as my book designer, Steve Straus, and my final proofreader, Susan Moore. Finally, to the people in my life who have always provided me with unconditional love and support so that I felt as if I had not one chance but a hundred chances: Ricardo Dapas, Toshinari Ishii, John Biggs, M. A. Biggs, Carla de Oro, and my parents. *Mil gracias.*

Professional Services

English & Associates is a team of independent professionals in Mendoza, Argentina, providing a variety of services to foreign corporations, investors, entrepreneurs, and educational institutions, including:

- **Study-Abroad Programs**—Two-week faculty-led courses in Mendoza that give university students the opportunity to visit the businesses and entrepreneurs profiled in *Expatriate Entrepreneurs in Emerging Markets*. Courses are designed to tie into existing business school curriculum so as to reinforce the global ideas and concepts taught in the classroom.
- **Seminars**—Presentations on life and work in emerging markets by the author and the entrepreneurs featured in this book.
- **Consulting**—One-on-one guidance from the author on investing or starting a business in Argentina.

For more information:

www.english-associates.com

or

info@english-associates.com

About the Author

David English is a recognized authority on foreign investment and entrepreneurship in Argentina. He has been featured or quoted in the *Financial Times, Fortune, Wine Enthusiast, Transitions Abroad, The Wall Street Journal*, CNN Money, *El Cronista Comercial*, and *La Nación*. As president of English & Associates, over the past ten years he has helped hundreds of investors and corporations from overseas do business in the Province of Mendoza. David is also founder of the Mendoza Expats Club. On a volunteer basis he manages the Mendoza-Nashville Symphony Orchestra Exchange Program and serves as the Mendoza coordinator for Sister Cities of Nashville. In addition, he organizes study-abroad and internship programs in Argentina for major universities around the world. David holds an English degree from the University of Tennessee in Knoxville and an MBA from Austral University in Buenos Aires.